Contents

KU-328-949

Introduction

I am not a professional folklorist but I do know that folklore is as much about the ordinary as about the extraordinary. Anyone, who has set himself to assist in collecting it will understand this. Perhaps I should say 'settled' rather than 'set' because in the process one will often have to settle oneself as comfortably as the surroundings allow, and listen or watch — become a pupil again as the informant takes over, with whatever degree of mastery he or she possesses.

A collector who expects to get the best an informant has to offer should possess patience, a sympathetic ear, commonsense, tact and a capacity for being disappointed without showing it. This is to simplify somewhat, of course, and these attributes, even when possessed to the highest degree, do not invariably guarantee success, but without them no beginning at all can be made. On occasion I admit that I have been bored even with the best of informants, perhaps through no fault of theirs (God knows what they may have thought of me) but I hope I have been sufficiently able to hide the fact.

There must be an after-sales service, as it were. It is wrong, I think, to have availed oneself of someone's time and effort (though willingly given) and then when what was sought has been secured to depart, never to see that informant again. Generosity imposes an obligation and though becoming onerous as one's circle of informants widens it is one which ought to be honoured. In many cases I have found that friendship, not duty, took me back time after time. In the case of Jimmy Armstrong that is surely the case.

Hospitable and willing from the beginning in as far as he was able he provided me, a Kerryman, with an insight into Co. Clare and its country people which I might not have achieved in years of living among them. His knowledge of his native district is extensive and detailed, as will be seen from the episodes related in this book (I may add here that the reader, necessarily a stranger to many of the places mentioned, will be greatly assisted, as I was, by an Ordnance Survey one inch map, sheet 133 [Sixmilebridge] which is roughly the area in question), and he is confident in the telling of his tales.

Another of his valuable attributes is his willingness to admit that the preternatural events he tells of may really have happened. This willingness allows him to tell his tales all the more convincingly, thereby showing the listener that these are no inventions but the happenings of a real, though strange, world. His anxiety to observe the impression he has made on the listener will, I hope, be apparent from the stories.

These stories themselves contain very varied material, from well-known folktales to the kind of local and personal incident which goes unnoticed except by a small circle of people. In them we see the reactionary landlords, the idiosyncratic, feared but respected clergymen, the local characters and the many others who lived in the Ireland of long ago; we see the trades and institutions that are no more; above all we see the common people of Ireland, as represented by this corner of Co. Clare, at work and at play, in sorrow and in joy. The social fabric of Ireland may be constantly ravelling and unravelling but the weavers of that fabric remain relatively unchanged.

If one agrees that all Jimmy Armstrong has told me is, in a way, remarkable, then equally significant is the fact that one such man's death can deprive an area of a large part of its oral tradition at one blow. I would hope that this book might encourage others, amateurs especially, to see this fact and act accordingly. The Folklore of Ireland Society has done, and is doing noble work but it cannot always be in time to save what could be saved and what needs so urgently to be saved.

Repeatedly throughout my talks with Jimmy Armstrong I asked him the question that must constantly be in the mind of anyone reading many of the episodes recounted in this book, i.e. could the local boyos and tricksters have been fooling him, knowing that he was disposed to be credulous where so-called preternatural happenings were concerned? He conceded that this was possible in some cases but that he would never know now. I have had to accept his stories in the same spirit; I will never know either. So I put them before the reader, knowing that the possibility of 'jocular fraudulence' exists, but confident that the manner in which the stories are told will carry the day.

Finally, a word on the text. I have recorded what I heard; no more, a little less. Editing has been necessary, and re-arrangement since not everything I recorded could be used in a book of this size and scope and some kind of order in the narrative is preferable to a haphazard approach. One thing I have not attempted to alter is Jimmy Armstrong's characteristic manner of expression. If there appear to be inconsistencies in usage, e.g. 'and' in some places, 'an'' in others; 'suppose' in some, 's'pose' in others it is due to my recording of these words as I heard them. I could have used discretion and standardised all such usages but I do not think such discretion is mine. That would be to falsify what I heard and would be unjust to the man who made this work possible, Jimmy Armstrong, though he would be the last to complain.

Edmund Lenihan

1. Background: Personal, Historical, Geographical

'I was born the second of May 1914 in Ballyroughan, about ten miles from Ennis. 'Twas at home most children were born that time. My father was a land steward for a Protestant in Daingean who was a landlord an' also a farmer. The difference between a land agent an' a land steward? Well, the agent would be for collectin' rents an' all that, but a steward would be a kind of a manager.

'There were two in the family, myself an' my brother, but he's dead now. I'm the last of the family. I was the favourite with my father an' he used to bring me with him wherever he'd be going. Now, he used take me to fairs but they were very tough places an' what I used to see about 'em was that some o' the people that were there, they were unmerciful to cattle. When the cattle would be tryin' to mix up with others they'd be floggin' 'em with sticks puttin' 'em back in their places an' all that. Well I hated to be lookin' at that kind o' thing.

'My father had a farm himself too an' he had tillage an' sheep, but when I was six or seven years of age he got out o' the sheep because they used to be gettin' tangled in the briars an' pullin' the wool off themselves. Then, when the young shoots would come out on the briars the sheep used to be pickin' 'em an' eatin' the bits o' wool as well with the result that it used to kill 'em. That's why he got out o' the sheep.

'My mother? Well, she was a hard-working woman, like a lot more women at the time. She used to churn; an end-over-end churn. 'Twas fairly big. 'Twould take about fifteen or sixteen gallons. An' clothes, now, when she'd wash 'em 'twas with a washboard in a timber tub. She used to do all home baking too, oven bread, made in a sixteen inch oven, the black iron oven. On an open fire, o' course.

'There wasn't much spent in the shops that time, only the bare necessities like tea an' sugar an' flour, things like that. You see, we'd kill our own pigs an' supply ourselves with turkeys an' geese too.

'I barely remember my grandmother. I was about five when she died. What sticks out in my memory about her was that she wore a brown, long dress an' she had a brown overcoat with a hood on it. 'Twasn't unusual to see them that time.

'I was ten when my father died, an' my mother died in December 1930. Then an aunt of ours came back from England to Ballyroughan to look after us.

'The farthest back I can remember is when my brother an' myself were goin' to Daingean national school. We used to have great fun there an' I was sorry to leave it. After that we went for two years to Saint Flannan's College in Ennis, from 1928 to 1930. We were never asked to do any work at home while we were at school but when my mother died we stopped school an' had to stay at home on the farm. I never worked anywhere else except at home an' I never travelled out a lot either. I had no money to go anywhere. In 1936 my aunt an' myself spent a fortnight at the Commercial Hotel in Lisdoonvarna, an' I was in England for a holiday in 1933, but that was all.

'My brother, now, he'd be content to sit down at home with a book, but I'd be out visiting the neighbours. An' that's where I got my interest in old stories. I used hear the old people around telling 'em an' somehow they appealed to me an' I followed 'em up. One old person might tell me, then, that there were other people that used to tell these old stories too, you see, an' I went on like that until I had most of 'em heard. An' as far as I know no one else o' my age had any interest in 'em around there.

'A lot o' the people that time were poor an' lived in small little houses, thatched, o' course. But the County Council put up slate houses for 'em then, the labourers' cottages, an' they did a lot o' good. There were a lot o' labourin' men that time. They'd get their day's hire mainly in the springtime settin' turnips an' cabbage an' that kind o' thing. Then in the summertime they'd be saving hay an' in the autumn they'd be cuttin' corn an' bindin' it for the farmers. They'd go on the dole then in the winter. The dole was small that time, you may say!

'Fishing? I spent, I s'pose, half my life fishing. 'Twas full o' lakes where we were. I could be naming 'em, I s'pose, for an hour for you, the local names o' the lakes. An' if you got a map they might have a different name altogether to the one I'd give you. There was a lot o' fishin' done in those lakes, mostly local people. There was pike an' bream an' tench there, plenty of 'em. I caught hundreds o' tench, an' they're a peculiar sort, a round lump of a fish. When you'd be fishing for 'em you'd have to feed the place the night before, an' the feed you'd put out for 'em was: mix about equal parts o' potatoes an' cabbage, an' the longer you'd have 'em boiled the better. If you had 'em boiled for six months that's the time they'd be good for the tench, when they'd be right sour. The general run o' the tench in the lakes was about six pounds.

'Another thing I was interested in was readin' gravestones, to see the names. An' that reminds me of a good one I heard. Denis Moloney had a bar an' a bakery in Quin one time — I'll tell you more about that too some other time — an' Michael Hogan, the Bard o' Thomond, came to Quin of a day an' he went in around the abbey takin' copies o' the names that were on the gravestones. When he had it done he came out to Denis Moloney's bar. There were some o' the lads around

11

Quin inside in the bar an' the Bard started talkin' to 'em about all the noble men that were all gone, that he was inside around the abbey takin' down their names off o' the gravestones. Wasn't it a great pity, he said, that all those fine noble men were gone. Denis Moloney was inside the counter an' he started laughin' at him.

'"Ah, Denis Moloney," sez he, "my friend, don't laugh, for Death took the wheat an' left but the chaff."

'That finished Denis laughin'.'

'Clocks were another thing I loved to be experimenting with. I used get 'em from the neighbours, broken ones, an' I'd keep at 'em until I'd get 'em going. I used put 'em in a press in my room at home an' I never felt it till I had forty-four of 'em, all varieties of 'em, an' they all going. An' d'you know what they were great for? When I'd go to bed at night, when I'd hear 'em tickin', the whole lot of 'em, I wouldn't be ten minutes in bed when I'd be sound asleep.'

"'Tis very hard to say, now, what was the biggest change I saw in my lifetime, but I would say that the person that invented the bicycle was far more clever than the person that invented the rocket that went to the moon. Consider now, that he never saw the bicycle before, an' that he put one wheel in front of another one, held together with a frame, an' that gadget, if you stood by the side of it an' pushed it along, 'twouldn't go the length of itself when 'twould fall, but cross your legs on it an' catch the handle-bars an' you can travel miles on it an' never fall. Isn't that surely a wonderful invention?

'The bicycle hastened the travelling, all right, but in another sense it did bad work. The people were healthier when they had to walk from here to Limerick.

They were more supple. There were some fierce journeys walked in the time before the bicycle. I heard of a man from Knappogue that walked to Galway an' back an' did it in two days. That's up on eighty miles. The most I walked myself was twenty miles in the one day, but I always had the bicycle so I had no need to walk too much.

'I was handy with bicycles. I built wheels for 'em, even. I studied the spokes, the way they were put in in the wheel. You could buy spokes at that time; I think 'twas two-pence each they were, two bob a dozen. Six dozen that was in the two wheels o' the bike, thirty-two spokes in the front wheel an' forty in the back wheel.

'I don't know, though, how many you'd want for the penny-farthing. 'Twas a strange-looking machine, all right. I saw one of 'em down in Newmarket an' I don't think I'd try ridin' it. There was no brake in the world on it, only use your leg if you could. The pedals were screwed onto the axle an' no such thing as a freewheel. You should let the pedals go with your legs goin' down a hill. There was a solid tyre on it, an' in the name o' goodness, you'd be nearly as well off to be above on a common horse-car. 'Twould shake you to pieces. But sure, hasn't everything to make a start somewhere? No matter what thing you'll look at around you won't you see that it had small beginnings an' came forward from that in its own way, all in good time.'

'I think to look forward is a good thing, not to be looking backwards all the time. But to go back in the past, we'll say, like the archaeologists do, to try an' find out how the people lived in them times, well, that's most interesting. But some people, then, they wouldn't bother their heads about that kind of thing; they'd want to live only for the future. An' there's nothing wrong with that either.

'But the big diggers an' JCBs an' bulldozers an' all the rest of it, they're goin' to smash what's there. 'Tis a pity. For instance, now, a JCB that you'd have makin' a drain, we'll say, through a field, sure 'tis unknown what might be there before it. Now, there might be maybe the greatest find of three or four thousand years in the field when this JCB might make bits of it. Well, that is wrong. 'Tis.

'Now, I saw it in fact — maybe you saw it yourself, Eddie, in the museum — the Ardagh Chalice. Wasn't that lovely! Beautiful! Well, how that was found, 'twas a man that was ploughin' with a pair o' horses, an' the plough stuck in a rock, an' o' course the pair o' horses, they kind of half lifted the rock. An' he got his spade an' dug around it to take it out of it altogether an' when he lifted it there were four slabs at the four sides of a hole, an' one on the bottom, an' this top one. Like a little box. An' the chalice was inside in it. 'Twas hidden there.

'D'you see the gold bracelets in the museum? Aren't they lovely! An' some o' them were got there below in Moohaun. Did you hear how 'twas found? Well, I'll tell you now.

'About half a mile beyond Willie Cullinan's there's a bridge over the railway. An' I suppose from the arch o' the bridge down to the railway 'twould be twenty feet anyway. It seems they had to cut through the crag to bring the railway level, d'you see. Well, when they went down below the bridge, towards Ballycar, the crag wasn't as high, but there was a height in the crag, a height of rocks, an' they had levelled down a bit of it. But they were gone down a good way below this height when the foreman he looked back an' he saw a big rock stickin' out o' the side o' this height. So he said to two or three of 'em to go back an' see about it. But they went back anyway with bars — crowbars — to take out this rock, an' when they rooted the rock it fell out, of course. Now, 'twas three or four feet from where they were

14

makin' the railway, an' when it fell out about a cartload of gold bars an' collars o' gold an' bracelets fell out after it. An' they didn't know what they were.

'But they filled their dinner bags with 'em, with these ornaments, rings an' bracelets an' God only knows what was in it. An' at dinner time, there were waterhens outside in Moohaun lake an' didn't they start peltin' the waterhens with the rings an' bars outside in the lake. They didn't know what they were. So, one of 'em, anyway, he had a dinner bag full of 'em an' he brought 'em in to a publican in Newmarket an' the publican he gave him a gallon o' whiskey for what he had. An' didn't the publican send 'em to the museum an' made a fortune out of 'em. An' 'twas that that put him an' his family on their feet. So, that's that.'

'But for the person that'd be interested in the past there's no shortage of things around here to keep him busy, between lakes an' castles an' forts an' wells an' God knows what else. Sure, a one'd want a life-time to see 'em all. Take castles, now. Isn't the place full of 'em. An' I'll tell you a story now about some o' them castles. MacNamara castles, they were.

'John MacNamara in Daingean, he had six brothers. An' he built six castles, one for each of his brothers. He built one in Daingean Breac, he built another in Ballymarkham, another in Knappogue, he built another at Rosroe an' one at Mountcashel an' one in Ballycullen. He made an agreement with his brothers that every fourth year they were to change about; like, the man that was in Daingean Breac had to go to Ballymarkham, an' the man in Ballymarkham had to go to Knappogue, an' the man in Knappogue had to go to Rosroe, the man in Rosroe had to go to Mountcashel, an' the man in Mountcashel to Ballycullen. But, the Ballycullen man then, you see, had to come back to Daingean Breac. An' that's the way they were to go every fourth year.

'Well, I think 'twas the eight year, the second turn, when the man in Knappogue refused to leave as it was the best of the six castles. So the other five brothers they attacked him, to put him out of it when he wouldn't keep to his agreement. He collected an army, an' the brothers collected another army an' they fought a fierce battle below in Knappogue. An' 'twas Augustine that was in Knappogue castle at the time, an' he got killed in the battle.

'Now, he was married to a sister of Henry Butler's in Castlecrin. An' the Butlers in Castlecrin, they were strict Catholics at the time. But in the reign of Elizabeth I, in order to hold Castlecrin, they turned Protestant. An' they held Castelcrin.

'But Isobel Butler was Augustine Mac's wife, an' she had a brother a priest in Maynooth or somewhere. In fact he was a bishop, an' president of some big college at the time. An' 'twas he wrote — you might often hear tell of it — the Penny Catechism. An' you could see written on the cover o' the catechism, "By the Right Rev. Dr James Butler D.D." An' the English soldiers, they told him that if he wanted to have Knappogue he could have it but to turn a Protestant. An' in order to hold the place he left the college an' turned a Protestant. He got married in Knappogue an' changed his name from James Butler to James Dunboyne. An' he was known after as Lord Dunboyne.

'The Dunboynes, they were there up to, I suppose, fifty or sixty years ago. An' then the Land Commission took it when the Dunboynes died away out of it.'

'Then, o' course, there's the standing stones. 'Twas at the back o' Carrahan school, there was a hill an' on top o' the hill there was a mass-rock an' during' the Penal times priests used to say mass on this rock.

16

'But there was a spy for the English at the time, an' the spy told the police in Tulla that the priest was in Carrahan sayin' the mass. So three policemen, they went out to arrest the priest, an' they were goin' up the hill, an' they saw all the people on top o' the hill. But, when they were about half way up the hill the three policemen turned into three stones. I heard that one all right.'

'Now, did you know that 'twas in Magh Adhair that the kings of Munster used to be crowned? An' the last king that was crowned there was Brian Boru.

'Now, there's a big mound there. I s'pose 'twould be about twenty feet high. Well, the top of it is flat, an' the last time I was there 'twas all small little blackthorn bushes on top of it, an' briars. Well now, when the kings used to be crowned there was a stone chair on top of it that the king would have to sit on. An' before the king would be crowned there — there's a basin, 'tis there yet, 'tis like as if 'twas made in the shape of an egg-cup. Now, 'tis wide on top, coming in narrow goin' down to the ground. Well now, on top of it there's a hollow and in that hollow 'twas the custom — I s'pose 'twould be handed down from the pagans — that the last born baby in the province would be brought an' killed, an' the blood of the baby put into this basin. An' the king, before he'd be crowned, would have to wash his hands in the blood an' take an oath solemnly swearing that during his reign he'd be completely innocent of the blood of his fellow-provincial people, as innocent as that baby was.'

'Well, I'll tell you a story about that place. Mikey Clune is livin' in a house just beyond it. Well, Mikey bought a horse from the travellers one time, an' the horse he bought from 'em, you'd want nearly a four-pronged fork after her to make her go. But anyway when he'd put her to the car an' tell her go on, she might be there for an hour before she'd start.

'But anyway, he put her to the car one day an' he was buildin' a wall between the road an' the yard an' the house. Well, around Magh Adhair there was a broken-down wall, an' the wall — you could see it yet — 'twas growin' moss an' grass an' everything through the stones. But he went over anyway, for to bring over a few loads of these stones to build the wall. He went over to Magh Adhair an' he filled his load o' stones. He told the mare to go on. The mare only looked back at him. He was at her an' at her to go when all of a sudden she started off in a trot, pulled the wheel o' the car up on the wall, up on the oul' broken-down wall, turned the car upside down an' broke the shaft of it.

'That finished Mikey with the stones from Magh Adair.'

'There's a river near it an' the bridge over it on the road 'tis called Hell's Bridge. I don't know why 'tis called that, but 'tis joining another river that's goin' down by Moymore an' comin' on by Brooke Lodge. About half way, now, between Hell's Bridge an' where 'tis joinin' the river there's a flat stone at the water's edge. Now, in the winter time the stone is covered, an' in the summer time you could go down on it. An' the print of two bare feet are on the stone. There must be a story followin' that too, but I don't know it.'

'Did I tell you about the Battle o' Rosroe? Well 'twas Paddy Scanlon that told me about it. There were two brothers of the MacNamaras, John "Fireball" MacNamara's two brothers, Finn an' Conn. Both of 'em were in love with the same girl, an' neither Conn knew that Finn was great with her, or Finn didn't know that Conn was great with her. But anyway, didn't Finn propose to her, an' married her, an' when Conn heard it didn't he rise a row with Finn. An' Finn gathered an army, an' Conn gathered an army, an' the two of 'em fought a fierce battle in Rosroe over the girl. An' Finn lost the sight of his eyes in the battle.

'But, they were holdin' a banquet, anyway, in Rosroe castle some time after. Didn't Conn go to the party an' he was goin' around dancin' with a girl. An' Finn was sittin' down. Then some fellow by the side of Finn, he said to him, "Here's Conn," sez he, "around dancin' with a girl, an' 'tis with your wife he's dancin'." An' what did Finn do? He pulled a dagger or a knife from under his coat an' stuck Conn with it in the back, an' killed him.

'An' below in Rosroe crag this very day you can see, now, in the middle o' the crag, a square hole. I s'pose 'twould be eight yards square. An' there's a low mound of earth around it, round the four sides of it, an' 'tis filled with loose stones. Well, 'twas supposed to be there that the people that were killed in the battle between the two MacNamaras were thrown in an' buried an' the stones thrown down on 'em. An' Michael Hogan, the Bard of Thomond, composed a poem about, "The Battle of Rosroe". But the story that I'm after tellin' you was there a long time before he ever wrote about it.

'As I mentioned the Bard, now, let me tell you another one about him. He used to live in Thomondgate in Limerick long ago, you know, an' he composed poems an' recitations about everywhere.

'But at one time he was workin' at Lord Dunraven's in Adare. One day, anyway, he said to Lord Dunraven that he'd like to compose a poem or a recitation about him, so did he mind?

'"No," sez Lord Dunraven to him, "provided," sez he, "that you'll send it to me before you'll get it made public."

'But anyway, Michael Hogan, he composed the poem

about Lord Dunraven an' he sent a messenger from Thomondgate out to Adare with the piece o' poetry. He didn't go himself, o' course, because he didn't know what way Lord Dunraven would take it. But anyway, Lord Dunraven, when he read the recitation, he was so pleased an' delighted with it that he gave the messenger forty pounds to bring back to Michael Hogan. But when the messenger went back to Thomondgate Michael Hogan wasn't there at all. He was out somewhere else, so the messenger gave the forty pounds to his mother.

'So, that evenin', anyway, when Michael Hogan came back she never opened her mouth about it, never said she got it, but kept it. In about a month after didn't Lord Dunraven send a messenger back to Thomondgate to know why Michael wasn't goin' to work, as he had him employed. Michael Hogan, he told the messenger from Adare that he'd go back Monday.

'He went back anyway, an' in two days after Lord Dunraven met him.

'"How is it," sez he, "that you never even acknowledged, or thanked me for, the nice present I sent you for the beautiful piece of poetry you composed about me?"

'"I got no present," sez Michael Hogan, "from you."

'But anyway, they left it so, an' when Michael Hogan went back home that night he was askin' his mother about what Lord Dunraven said to him. There an' then she admitted it. She said she got it an' she kept it.

"Well," sez Michael Hogan to her,

"I must go to a priest," sez he, "an' get holy anointed,
For in this world I am disappointed.
I must leave this world an' go to another
For in this world you couldn't trust your mother."

'I heard another poem he composed, too "Pat O'Leary an' his Mountain Mary" was the name of it. I don't know the poem but I know the story behind it, an' that story was there, too; before Hogan ever went at it.

'John Mac had this workman in Daingean; Pat O'Leary was his name. An' I heard that at the time there used to be fairs in Aonach. That was near Kilkishen, about a mile an' a half from Kilkishen. But sometime, anyway, in the mornin', I suppose 'twould be about three or four o' clock in the mornin', John Mac had Pat O'Leary told to go to the fair of Aonach with a cow for him. So Pat said he would. But, he was goin' down at Cullane lake when the cow turned in towards the lake. Pat went in after her o' course. The cow took a drink out o' the lake, anyway, an' when she was finished Pat turned her out again. But didn't he pick a bit of a stick that was growin' near the lake to drive her out on the road an' went away to the fair, an' thought no more of it.

'Now, a lot o' people knew Pat O'Leary around Kilkishen an' around Daingean, an' people from Daingean were at the fair. But when Pat went to the fair, anyway, they were lookin' at him, an' he sez to one of 'em, "What in the name o' God," sez he, "are ye lookin' at?" "Where in Heaven's name," sez this man to him, "did you get the big whisker?" "I have no whisker," sez Pat to him. "Didn't I shave myself before I came out this mornin'."

'He put his hand up to his face an' there the whisker was. An' d'you know what happened? When he went in to turn the cow from the lake he thought 'twas only about three or four minutes that the cow was takin' the drink o' water. An' wasn't it that day twelve months before that he went to the fair of Aonach. He was in Tír na nÓg for a whole year an' he thought 'twas only about four minutes.

'But the stick that he picked to drive out the cow with, I heard that any row or faction fight he was ever in after that he had only to swing that stick an' they'd fall like flies around him. That was no ordinary stick, either.'

'Strange things in lakes? Well, I'll tell you, now, about something I saw myself, although I don't know would you call it strange or not.

'Did you ever see a crannóg? Well, there's a crannóg in Rosroe lake. 'Twas excavated by Joseph Raftery in 1937. I used to be in there when they were at it. They got the part o' the floor of a dwelling house. They got two gold armlets, two gold bracelets an' an earthenware jug too. I saw the whole lot of 'em. They were lovely. Lovely. There were interlaced lines drawn out on 'em, an' the jug, 'twas some sort of leaves that were on the jug. 'Twasn't broken. For all the world, now, 'twas like an earthenware flowerpot, only wide in the middle, d'you know what I mean, an' narrow above an' below, an' a spout an' a handle an' all on it.

'An' when they were finished there they left the place, now, as they started. No! They covered nothin'. Left everything open.

'Now, the kind of place the crannóg was in. You'd go over by the edge of a bog, an' beyond the bog you could see the lake. Well, the crannóg, then, d'you see, was a sort of a peninsula that was goin' out in the lake. An' between the mainland an' this peninsula there was a formation, I could say, of a trench.

'Sylvester Boland that found it. 1935, I think it was, that he was shootin' duck over in the lake, an' a flock o' duck got up an' he fired into the flock of 'em, two barrels. Two of 'em fell outside on this island. Now, 'twas in the winter time, in the month o' November, an' he had to take off his boots an' tuck up his trousers to go out to 'em. An' when he went out he saw all these stakes driven down in the water. They were as rotten as bread steeped in water. But didn't he see what he thought was the cover of a tin can stickin' up out o' the mud, an' he pulled it, an' what was it only an axe.

'He sent it to the museum. 'Twas a bronze axe of the early bronze age. An' two years later they came an' excavated it.

'Now, you might think that was a strange thing to get in a lake, but I'll tell you one, now, about a lake, one that's a lot stranger than that.

'D'you remember me tellin' you a while ago about John "Fireball" MacNamara below in Daingean? Well, he was also known as the Lord of Clancullen. An' he had a workman in Daingean whose name was Pat O'Leary — sure, I was tellin' you that, wasn't I? Well, Pat O'Leary was workin' with John Mac for years. An' John Mac was a great huntsman, an' he decided one time to go to the fair in Limerick. At that time there used to be Munster horse fairs in Limerick, an' John Mac decided to go to the fair to buy a hunter. So himself an' Pat O'Leary, they went to the fair an' John Mac selected a lovely white mare.

'They brought her back to Daingean an' let her out in the field. Next day she was gone. They got her up beyond around Tulla; that'd be about five or six miles away. They brought her back again an' put her into the field. Next day she was gone again. They got her below Kilkishen. They brought her back again, put her into a house with a chain an' a hasp on the door. The next day she was gone.

'So, the mare had their heart broken. An' what did they do? John MacNamara decided to get her in foal an' that might stop her. But for about a month, say, before she had the foal, an' about a month after, that was as long as she stayed. Then herself an' the foal started goin'. An' she had their heart broken in Daingean. They decided they could get no good of her so John Mac decided to go to the Munster fair in Limerick again to sell her, herself an' the foal.

'But, the night before the fair he dispatched Pat

O'Leary, ridin' on the mare, an' the foal after her, to Limerick. Anyway, goin' down at Scart — 'tis above Kilkishen — the mare wheeled in towards Cullane lake. An' Pat O'Leary tried to pull her out, but she still persisted in goin' in. So he thought then 'twas thirsty she was, an' he let her off. She went out along a rocky peninsula that was goin' out into the lake an' when she got out to the end of it she took a jump. An' there's a flat rock now, outside the top o' the peninsula, an' in the summer time the top of it is dry, an' in the winter time the water is over it. But the mare took a jump from the top o' the peninsula an' landed on this rock outside, an' out o' that out on the water an' Pat O'Leary was on her back. I heard that in a rough, gruff voice she spoke, an' said, "I'll appear every seven years with my rider."

'The foal jumped in after her an' down they went.

'There were more people goin' to the fair an' they heard her, an' that day seven years didn't they watch again in the same peninsula, an' the mare an' the foal came up all right, but in Cullane Lawn, which is a good piece away from where they were. But naturally, when there was no one there, o' course, she went into the lake again.

'That day seven years again they watched in Cullane Lawn, hundreds o' people, an' the mare an' foal came up on the Lawn an' Pat O'Leary on her back. So, they went to surround the mare an' foal, but the mare got into the lake with Pat O'Leary. They prevented the foal goin' into the lake, an' where did the foal go only up Cullane Turret Hill, up to the top o' the hill. An' he took a jump from the top o' the Turret Hill an' landed on the top o' Ballyroughan Hill. That'd be a distance of about a mile. Well, the foal landed on a rock that was on top o' Ballyroughan Hill an' out o' that he jumped into the Tírín lake.

'Now, my grandfather, when he was buildin' a stable

in Ballyroughan, didn't he bring a piece o' the rock where the foal landed an' put it inside the door of the stable. An' 'tis there to this day. You can see the print of three small hoofs. It appears that the stone wouldn't fit in the wall with the fourth one. But they broke it off it, the print o' the fourth hoof. The three hoofs, though, three small hoofs, are there to this day in the rock inside the stable door, at the right-hand side as you go in. So that's that story.'

'While I think of it now I must tell you another one about a lake. The McDonalds used to live in Newhall House an' they used to make wine in that house. Now, there was a cellar in the house an' when they'd make the wine they used to put it down in the cellar. But, 'twas missing out o' the cellar maybe once a fortnight, or once a week. So they watched it, an' 'twas at night time, o' course, it used to go. But this night they saw, coming up from the lake a mermaid, coming up out o' the lake an' goin' into the cellar an' drinkin' some o' the wine, an' goin' back into the lake again. So the watchmen that were keepin' a lookout, they were tellin' the owner, McDonald, what they saw and didn't he stay up to watch her with a double-barrel gun. An' she came up out o' the lake an' into the cellar, an' he let her alone until she was goin' back again to the lake. Then, when he saw her goin' he blocked her way an' tried to stop her o' goin' for the water. But she went a different way from her usual track, an' she was goin' from him. So he fired at her an' wounded her. But she got back into the lake in spite of it an' as she went from the house to the lake she cut a trench with her tail. 'Tis there yet. You can see it yourself! But, she died in the lake from the effects o' the wound, an' every seven years that lake turns the colour o' wine. An' I heard that there wasn't much luck in that house ever since.

'But there's a vault under the abbey — Newhall

Abbey — near the lake, an' if you went into the vault you'll hear a drop o' water falling into more water from the roof o' this vault. An' you won't see it at all, only hear it. 'Tis drop, now, like PINK! PINK! PINK! that sort o' way, falling down. An' I heard that if it fell on you you'd be bald ever after. More people say 'twould kill you. I don't know. But you won't see it at all, or know where it is; only if you go to the door you'll hear it.

'What's the connection between that an' the mermaid? Well, the man that told me that story, he said that 'twas supposed to be the mermaid's drop. Whatever he meant by that I don't know.'

'Wait one minute now. I'll tell you one more before you go. One thing brings down another an' while we're talkin' about water I'll tell you this one before I forget it. I heard that in Feenish Island in the mouth o' the Fergus, where the Fergus joins the Shannon, there was a giant long ago. Now, where the Fergus joins the Shannon, 'twould be about a mile an' a half west of where the present airport is, that's the townland of Rinn Eanna. Well, in that townland there was a pirates' town in olden times, and in Feenish there was a giant an' another one in the pirates' town. But the two, at one time, they rose a row, an' the giant at Feenish he came in to attack the giant in Rinn Eanna. Bedad, when he came in the giant in Rinn Eanna ran from him towards Stonehall an' Carraig Eala. But the giant from Feenish followed him an' when he came to the top of Carraig Eala hill the giant from Rinn Eanna would be about a quarter of a mile ahead of him. So the giant from Feenish, he picked up a rock that he got on top o' the hill, an' his wife was after him. An' when he picked up the rock he let fly after the giant from Rinn Eanna. Then the wife, when he let the big rock fly that he picked up, she handed him a smaller one to let after him again. But, the big one landed about a quarter of a mile away from where he was, an' the small one landed on top of it. So, the big rock would be about eight ton weight an' the small one about two ton, an' the two of 'em are there to this day, in a small little field at the right o' the road as you'd be going over to Carraig Eala church. They're inside in a field there.'

2. At Work and at Leisure.

'Indeed I did know a lot of handy men in my day, Eddie, an' every one of 'em good at his own game. Take killing pigs, now. In years past we used to kill 'em at home. There was a man going round, a local man from Bally-markham, an' he used to kill for several o' the neighbours.

'Well, I'll tell you now how he'd go about it. Now, the night before killing the pig you wouldn't feed him at all, or that morning, an' naturally, o' course, the pig'd be hungry. But, I used to hate seeing anything killed, even the poor pig, so I usedn't to go near 'em at all when they'd be killin'. But my man that used to do the killin', he'd get a rope, a horse-reins, an' put a running loop on the end of it, an' get a bit of, I could say, mess in a bucket, boiled potatoes. Throw the loop o' the rope into the pig's trough an' throw the bit o' food on top of it. Of course when the pig'd be eatin' the food an' he so hungry naturally he'd put the rope into his mouth; he'd eat the rope as well as the mess. An' my man, he'd have the end o' the rope, d'you see, an' when the poor pig'd put the rope into his mouth my man'd pull. The running knot, o' course, on the rope would close around the pig's nose, an' the more the pig would pull the more the knot would squeeze.

'But anyway, two more would go behind the pig an' they'd hunt him into another house where there'd be a table an', I could say, a sheep-dipping tub o' boiling water. Now, when they'd hunt the pig into the house my man would get a hatchet, a four-pound hatchet, an' one crack into the pig's head, between the pig's eyes, with the poll o' the hatchet, an' the pig'd fall down. Now, three or four men then, would catch the pig an' up on the table with him an' stick him with a knife through the heart. An' the blood would gush out, an' have a bucket to hold it. After a few minutes the pig was dead.

'Then, the pig was gone into this tub o' boiling water, the dead pig. Leave him in it for about twenty minutes to scald him. Up on the table then an' you'd have knives, about four people with four knives that were sharpened nearly as sharp as a razor, to scrape the hair off the pig.

'Well, more people, how I heard they used to do it was, there'd be a beam o' timber across the house an' they'd have a pulley on the beam, an' they'd tie the pig's hind legs with a rope, an' put the rope through the pulley an' pull up the pig — dead o' course — an' when they'd have the pig's head within a foot o' the ground they'd put down a fire o' straw under the pig an' the blaze o' the straw would burn the hair off the pig.

'Well, 'tis the boiling water that we always used, although I wouldn't be there at all to see it. Then, o' course, my man would open the pig an' take out his guts. They'd be cleaned an' washed, an' filled with the pig's blood, an' boiled. I think there used to be onions an' oaten-meal an' things put in with the blood. Everyone had their own kind of a mix, you know.

'But the funny part of the story was, there wasn't a week in the year but a heifer or a bullock or a sheep would die on that man that used to do the killin', an' there was no account for it. But he was tellin' this neighbour of his how they were dyin' an' the neighbour said to him,

'"Tell me," sez he, "do you charge at all," sez he, "for the killin' o' the pigs?"

'"I do not," sez he. "Sure what would I charge an' they neighbours?"

'"Well now," sez he, "your luck is goin'. If you only charged a penny," sez he, "your cattle or sheep," sez he, "wouldn't be dying."

'But after that he used to charge a shilling for to kill the pigs, an' the cattle an' sheep stopped dying.

'But anyway, to get back to the meat o' the pig. Generally he used to make four pieces of each side, cut the pig in two an' make four pieces out of each side. What used to be done then, get a barrel, a timber barrel, a forty-gallon barrel. Well now, put a layer of salt, I suppose about two inches of salt, in the bottom o' the barrel. Put a layer o' meat down on that, about another two inches o' salt down on the meat; another layer o' meat on top o' that salt — the barrel would take about two pieces o' meat, d'you see, in the breadth of it. But, you had four layers o' meat, an' five layers o' salt between the meat an' over the meat.

'Well then, when that was done, get a bucket o' boiling water. Now, put a big potato into the bucket o' boiling water, a raw potato. The potato would sink in the water to the bottom o' the bucket. Keep adding salt to that water until the potato would float. When 'twas strong enough throw it into a barrel o' meat an' salt an' leave it there, an' after about a week the whole thing, the water, 'twould be raised over the meat.

'Now, leave it there for six weeks, covered in the barrel. But, after six weeks take it out of it, put it somewhere to drain an' then hang it, an' you had meat for the year. 'Twould dry out hard.

'Some people, then, used to smoke the meat. But, what I heard that you'd want for smoking the meat, you'd want a house with no windows in it. An' you'd want to leave the meat, d'you see; you'd want a sort of an iron grate that you'd leave the meat on, supported from the ground. An' there'd be no windows in the house, an' I suppose you'd nearly want an iron door in it as well. But maybe a right strong timber one'd do. Now, where you'd leave the meat, up on the grate, put a fire o' straw under the grate an' light it an' shut the door.

Leave it there for two days. The smoke o' the straw'd be inside in the house. After two days then, you see, the smoke'd be gone through it.'

'Did you ever hear the saying "As dry as a lime-burner's hat?" Well, there was good reason for that saying, an' I'll tell you what I know about it now. This is how they used to burn the lime, an' I was in the fillin' of a kiln myself.

'Now, below in the bottom o' the kiln 'twas lined with firebrick. The kiln was built with limestone, o' course, an' lined with firebrick round. An' I s'pose 'twould be about eight feet in diameter. Well now, the brick below in the bottom, 'twas tapered in, brought in narrow. An' then, o' course, 'twas widened goin' up until 'twas eight feet in diameter. Now, when you'd be fillin' the kiln there was, I could say, a gate that was below in the bottom of it. You could pull out this iron thing, an' o' course, you had a crook to pull it out when 'twould be hot. Well, you put in this gate, or grate, that had a very narrow space between the bars, an' four barrowfulls o' coal in on top o' that first. Now, on top o' that you put about a foot thick of the bright grey limestone, in big lumps. But on top o' that, then, you put about another foot of coal. An' fill it that way alternatively with coal an' stone, up to the top, an' when you'd have it filled to the top cover it with sheets o' galvanised. You could leave a few stones down on the sheets o' galvanised to keep 'em from blowin' away with the wind. Now, you had four barrowfuls o' coal below in the bottom then, an' you start the coal, with turf; anything! Sticks or turf. Anything that'd start, light the coal. Now, when that coal would take fire, the blaze would go through the stones an' catch the coal that'd be on top of 'em with the result that it had to burn, the stones had to burn. When the coal on top o' them, then, again you see, would

31

catch fire that would go up through the other layer, right up to the top. 'Twould take it a week to burn. I suppose one full o' the kiln, you'd get about seven or eight ton. You would. But I would say, though, that 'twas a dear way of making lime. Turf wouldn't do. 'Twouldn't be hot enough, d'you see, to burn the stones. Although, in Ballyroughan, now, there was a turf-kiln. My grandfather had it there. An' it used to do the job. It must be stone-turf he had for it, though.

'The heat out o' that kiln, o' course, would be severe for the man tendin' it an' that's why the saying "As dry as a lime-burner's hat" was there. Thirsty work it was, I tell you.'

'Another tough job was breakin' stones for the road. That was for the old roads, d'you see, before they were tarred. Them roads now, mind you, used to smooth down after a while. But they'd be full o' potholes in the winter. But the stones they used to break for the road, there used to be nearly a pound weight in 'em. An' broken with the hand, o' course. They used get paid by the yard. Patsy Griffy in Kilcornan was tellin' me that 'twas three shillings a yard for breakin' 'em. 'Twas three feet long, three feet wide an' three feet high, a box made that measurement, an' the full o' that was for three bob. 'Twas hard money.'

'Did you ever see the roof being put on a house? I'll bet you did! Well now, there's no comparison between the way they do it now an' the way I saw it done long ago. The roofs long ago, of course, were thatched, an' the rafters that were holding up the thatch, they were, I could say, just naturally cut from as straight a tree that they could get, an' they were some of 'em crooked an' more of 'em kind o' straight. Well then, on top o' them there were what the old people used to call rubberies.

They were branches about as round as a man's arm an'
they were split; some of 'em, I suppose, would be about
four feet long. An' how they used to split 'em I don't
know, but they'd split 'em through the middle, an' they
were put across the rafters, I suppose about maybe
fifteen of sixteen inches apart. Then on top o' them
there were bog scraws, scraws got out of a bog. Now, 'tis
only in a very odd bog that you'd get 'em. Some o' the
bog scraws, they'd break easy. They'd search for 'em
until they'd get scraws that'd be as tough as leather, an'
'tis with hay-knives they'd cut 'em. They'd bring those
then to put up on the rubberies, an' how they used to put
'em up, the grassy side in an' the earthy side out. Well,
when they'd put up the layer o' scraws on the rubberies
on top o' the rafters they'd sew 'em. Now, you might
ever hear, Eddie, of twine that was known as spun yarn.
'Twas a coarse, brown twine, like a light rope. Well
now, they'd sew the scraws to the rubberies with that,
an' they had a thatchin' needle for the job. 'Twas a rod
of iron about four feet long, with an eye on the end of it.
An' the eye, I suppose, would be about two inches
across for the twine to go into.

'Now, how the sewing was done, there'd have to be a
man inside an' a man outside. He didn't know very well,
of course, where to put down the needle from the outside. Remember now, the rubbery, 'twould be five or six
feet long, an' they'd roll the scraws to bring 'em, an' put
'em up along the rubberies.

'Well, the man outside that had the needle, he'd drive
the needle in through the scraw with the twine in the eye
of it. The man inside would take the twine out o' the eye
o' the needle. The man outside would pull out the
needle again, an' stick it in in another place. Now, the
second time he might stick it maybe in the wrong place
an' the man inside would tell him he was wrong, to pull it
out again an' keep down farther. He had to put it, d'you

see, below the rubbery an' when he'd put it in there the man inside would put the twine into it, an' the man outside would pull it out again with the twine. They'd go on like that, in an' out.

'Well now, when they had all their scraws up, all the rubberies covered with the scraws, they had wheaten straw ready. That'd be scutched, o' course, because they couldn't put it through a threshin' machine; 'twould break all the straw. Now, they had that, an' they had every rush of it side by side, in the sheaves. They'd open their sheaves when they had all their scraws up. They'd start at one end o' the house an' leave down as much as they were able to take in their fist of this wheaten reed.

'Now, they had scollops and hazel rods about two feet long, an' they'd twist the rods in the middle, an' the idea of twistin' 'em was the way they wouldn't break. Where you'd twist the rods, they'd bend like a staple. Anyway, when they'd put down their fist of wheaten reed they'd have this scollop twisted an' they'd put down a leg of it at either side of the handful of reed. Well now, another handful o' reed down by the side o' that; another rod down on that. They'd continue all along the bottom of the roof that way.

'The second row of reed, then, handfuls o' reed, they'd have to come half way between the two bottom ones, an' let it down about three quarter way or half way down the first row. An' they'd put the rods on 'em the same as they did the first row. They'd continue on that way up to the top. Well now, they couldn't do, o' course, only about seven or eight feet of it at the time because they'd have to be changin' the ladder.

'When they'd have all their roof thatched with the reed, in order to ornament it they'd put the thick hazel rods in a row, one after the other, below at the bottom. They'd have thin rods then, that they'd twist to hold them in position. They'd have these, I s'pose, about a foot an' a half apart, an' between those 'twas the very same as the letter X. An' they'd hold 'em at the four ends with four light little rods, an' when 'twas done 'twas very nice. They'd do the same above at the top at both ends, top an' bottom o' the roof.

'A good thatcher, now, 'twould take him about a fortnight. 'Twould. An' for that thatchin' job they used generally get a pound a day when I knew 'em, an' that was good wages.

'Sure, every parish had a thatcher that time, an' three or four of 'em. Where used they get the scollops? Well, generally the person that would own the house would get the scollops for 'em. I remember splittin' scollops. An' 'tis easy split 'em: an ordinary bread-knife. Now, the end o' the scollop, you had to cut it from one side, one side only, an' cut it in a slope, about an inch long, an inch of a cut. When you had it cut that way, across the end of it, just sink the blade o' the knife the depth of itself into the end o' the rod. Now, hold the knife an' that end, an' across your knee, about two inches from the blade o' the knife you bend the rod with the knife in it an' the crack will go right straight from the knife to where you bent it. You push the knife then as far as the end o' that bend of that split. Now, about two inches again you bend the rod again, an' the crack will follow to where you bend it again.

'Then the thatcher had a comb for combin' down the straw, an' the comb was, I could say, a block o' timber with four inch nails, a row o' four inch nails in it.

'An' then he had a knife, for cutting the end o' the reed at the bottom, to bring it even. That'd be just above the wall o' the house. An' how it had to be cut, Eddie, outside the wall; at the top o' the thatch, now, 'twas longer than inside near the wall. 'Twould have to be cut flat in at an angle.'

'Another thing I heard about is bittling. I s'pose this would happen before the soap came out for washin' clothes. The women, before the soap came out, when they'd want to wash clothes, they'd select a slow-flowing river or a stream where the water'd be flowing slow; not too slow, you know, only just what'd wash the dirt away. If 'twas flowin' fast when they'd be washin' the clothes 'twould sweep the clothes. They wanted it in such a way as that the clothes would remain in the river, an' at the same time the dirt would be washed away.

'An' they'd prefer it with a rocky or a sandy bottom. They'd get a flag then, get the men to get a flag — an' the bigger they could get the flag the better they'd like it. If they got one about eight foot square they'd prefer it. They'd put down the flag in the bottom o' the river where the water would be flowin' slowly. They'd get a bucket o' the water then an' wet the clothes well in the bucket o' water. They'd spread 'em out on the flag in the stream, the thicker they could get 'em the better, a foot thick. An' there'd want to be about a foot an' a half of water over the flag. They had, then, what they called a bittle-to. 'Twas a handle about four feet long, an' at the lower end of it there was a round piece o' timber, say, about a foot in diameter, or sixteen inches, with the lower surface of this bit o' timber curved. 'Twould be like a saucer, now, the bottom of it, but the top of it would be flat, where 'twould be on to the handle. Well, they had a long nail then, or a long screw screwed through this piece o' timber onto the handle, an' the handle had to be in the exact middle of this circular piece o' timber.

'When they'd have the wet clothes down on the flag then, a woman would take off her boots an' stockings an' go down on the clothes, or by the side o' the clothes, an' pound 'em with this bittle below in the river. Every bit o' dirt that was on 'em, the slow-flowing water would wash it away. An' they'd wash sheets in that, Eddie, as white as if they had soap to wash 'em. An' in various parts of rivers an' streams the bittling flags are there to this day.

'When last did I see it done? I never saw it done, only heard about it. I'm not all that old, you know!'

'That's a thing, I'd say, you never saw working was a winnowing machine. They were used up to about 1950, I s'pose. I remember well the one that was in Bally-roughan. 'Twas written on the side of it: "Manufactured by J. Atkins & Sons, Cork".

'This machine, o' course, was worked by hand. What it looked like was a press that you'd have left down on its side. Made o' timber, o' course, but the axles were iron. An' the length o' the machine, 'twould be about eight feet long and the inside measurement was about three feet to the best o' my knowledge. Now, the bottom of the machine was open. Then, a three by three at the back was holed an' an iron bushing put into the hole for a round iron axle. Onto this axle there were two discs, round discs of timber, an' the timber that was used in it was elm because the elm timber, 'twas not too easy to split it. Around the edge of these two discs there were six mortises sank an' every one of 'em an inch square. Then there were six rods, square rods, an inch square, an' they were driven into these six mortises. So the two discs were held rigidly, I could say, at equal distance from the sides of the machine.

'The square rods, then, they were projecting about fifteen inches from the discs, an' there was light timber then — nailed across these six projecting rods. Behind the machine, at the right-hand side, there was a cog-wheel put on the end o' the axle. An' over that cog-wheel at the end o' the axle, I could say the beater axle, to create the wind, there was another cog-wheel about a foot in diameter, an' the bottom one would be about four inches. Now, there was a thread in the axle of the bigger cog-wheel that you could screw on a handle to it. At the other side, then, of the beater axle there was a bevelled cog-wheel put on it. The cogs in the wheel were at an angle o' forty-five degrees. From that out along the left-hand side o' the machine there was an iron rod, say, a half inch or three quarter inch in diameter an' that rod was goin' in through a slot in the boards an' goin' on to a shaker inside.

'Now, to describe the shaker for you. 'Twas two boards, an' these boards, I think they were elm as well. They'd be about sixteen inches square. Now, in the middle of these boards there was a groove cut about half the thickness o' the board, an' the board would be about one an' a half inches thick. The boards were, say, about sixteen inches apart. Well, there was one groove cut in the middle of the board, another groove cut about two inches below that, an' the idea of these grooves was to hold the two sieves.

'The bottom o' the shaker-boards, then, they were wider behind than they were in the front, an' there was a groove cut slant-wise along to hold what was known as the screen. Now, this screen was in a timber frame an' all it was was perforated tin. And, to hold in the two top sieves there was a chute of iron about four inches along with a washer on the inner end. An' between the washer an' an iron bar, which was holed for it, there was a spring.

'In the front of this chute there was a grip for your hand — you could put your four fingers into an eye that was in it an' pull it out with your hand an' turn it. Inside this hand grip there was a long piece of iron, 'twould be about six inches long. Now, when you turn the chute, pull it out an' put tension on the spring. Now, the bit of iron, you'd turn it also an' 'twould catch the two sieves

an' 'twouldn't let 'em come out. At the back o' the sieve there were two straps of iron — an' the two sieves, when you'd push 'em in they'd go in comfortably against these two straps of iron. When you'd turn your hand chute, then, outside they were held securely. Under these two sieves the screen was on a timber frame an' 'twas only a sheet of perforated tin. Now, that was sloped backwards.

'On top o' the machine, then, there was a square funnel. On this square funnel there was a square hole at the bottom of it. At the back of the shaker, then, there was a place left for a cross-board an' the cross-board was about, say, a quarter of an inch under this square funnel. Now, in the front of the square funnel there was a board on a slide, that you could let up an' down as you wanted to let down the corn fast or slow. If you let down the corn too fast 'twould choke the sieve, an' 'twouldn't blow the chaff out of it. An' then o' course, if you let it down too slow that was only a waste o' time. Anyhow, the mesh in the top sieve was a bigger mesh than the bottom one. There were four sieves, in fact. Now, there was a sieve for flax, barley an' oats, an' the barley sieve would also do wheat. But the oaten sieve, 'twas a bigger mesh than the other two on account o' the grain of the oats being longer than the wheat or the barley, to give it a chance of goin' down.

'At the back of the screen there was a slanted floor put in the machine so that when the corn would go down through the two sieves on to this screen the wind from the beaters was kind o' blowin' the corn against the screen, an' at the same time the screen was vibratin'. So the wind used to delay the corn against the screen, an' whoever invented it had a bit o' brains, because when the wind was blowin' the corn against the slanted screen small seeds o' weeds like thistle seeds an' dock-leaf seeds an' dandelion seeds an' God only knows what different kinds o' seeds, they'd go through the screen, whereas the grain o' the corn couldn't go through it. The grains o' corn would slide down along the screen, onto this floor that was to take 'em, an' naturally, when the floor was slanted, they'd go out at the back o' the machine, down on the ground as well.

'Now, two men would work the machine, one twisting it an' the other feeding it. The man that'd be feeding it, except he had a helper to take away the clean corn from the back of it, he'd have to stop an' take away the corn himself. Now, the shaker, I described it for you already, but 'tis like the rest o' the winnowing machine; you'd actually want to see it to know exactly how it worked. Well, two men with that winnowing machine, they'd do about two hundred stone o' corn in a day. An' they'd have to bag it themselves after.

'Now, before those machines were invented, when people would want to do the winnowing they should have a house with two doors in it. An' they couldn't clean the corn, o' course, except there was a good breeze blowin', an' the breeze would have to be blowin' in one o' the doors. Then they'd open the two doors an' spread a bit o' sheet or something on the floor, an' they'd get their bucket o' corn an' let it down slowly down on the sheet an' let the wind blow the chaff out of it. Sure I s'pose 'twouldn't half blow it out of it.

'I saw the flail working too. 'Twas made of ash and holly, an' the names that I heard for the parts o' the flail were that the ash was the handle an' the holly was the beater. This beater was also called the *buailteán*. The two of 'em used to be joined with a piece o' leather called a *gad*.

'Now, I'll tell you how 'twas used, an' I even saw it used. There was an old man below in my home place an' that old man was from Ralahine. His name was John Henchy. He was there in my father's time. An' there was a house at the end o' the yard an' the house was thatched an' my great grandfather used to live there one time. Now, my father used to continue to thatch it for a few years an' he used to sow wheat, mainly for the thatch for this house.

'But this old man from Ralahine, I saw him once or twice flailing the wheat. The way he used to do it, he'd get maybe two sheaves o' wheat, thick; you know what I mean, get about a dozen sheaves o' wheat an' put the dozen, or maybe more, one after the other with the seed of the wheat facing the one direction. Now he'd get maybe fifteen or sixteen more sheaves an' he'd put the seed of that down on top of the seed of the first row. He'd get then fifteen or sixteen sheaves more an' he'd leave 'em down on top o' them again with the seed facin' the one direction again. Now, the butts o' the sheaves would be separated. They wouldn't be facing each other; only the heads. There'd be two sheaves, then, one on top o' the other, or maybe where the two sheaves would meet side by side the one on top of 'em might come between the two bottom ones. So, when he'd have his two layers o' wheat down he'd get his flail an' he'd stand at the butt end of one of the rows of sheaves. An' he'd wheel the *buailteán* over his head the length of the handle from him, an' when he'd wheel the *buailteán* he'd lower the handle so as that 'twould come down level on the seed o' the wheat, the full length down on the seed o' the wheat. An' he'd hit it maybe a hundred times, or maybe more. He'd do that for the length of his fifteen or sixteen sheaves, an' then he'd have to feel the corn to know was the seed gone out of it. An' sometimes it wouldn't, an' more times it would, but he'd have to continue beating it until he'd get all the seed out of it.

'Well now, when he'd have that lot done he'd put down about thirty more sheaves, fifteen down first an' fifteen more down on top of 'em, an' continue on that way until he'd have enough done for the thatch of this old house. But after some years o' doin' this my father, God rest his soul, he decided to put galvanised outside the thatch. So that finished the flailing o' the wheat.

'This old man, John Henchy, he told me that before the flail came in how they used to do the wheat for thatch was to scutch it. And, the scutching was, get a box maybe three feet high an' put a big rock on top o' this box, an' slash the seed off o' the sheaves against the rock to knock it out of it.'

'A thing that was done in every farmer's house long ago was butter-making. An' 'tis a churn they'd have for making the butter. Well now, I won't tell you how they used to make the butter; that was simple enough. What I'll tell you is how butter was taken. Piseógs, you know.

'This woman I knew, 'twas reported that she used to take people's butter. But, the woman in a house where I used to call, one Friday she was makin' the churn an' she started the churn about eleven o' clock. But she was at it until dinner-time anyway, an' she left it there an' got the dinner ready for the family. After the dinner, anyway, she started the churn again, an' about five o' clock in the evenin' 'twas like suds that were inside in the churn. She sent her son to Quin for the priest an' he came.

'Now, what he did was: the churn was inside in the middle o' the kitchen; 'twas one o' the dash churns. But, he went over to it, anyway, an' he asked her to take the cover off the churn an' give him a teaspoonful o' salt. She gave him the teaspoonful o' salt an' he blessed it an' threw it into the churn. She put on the cover again an' she took the staff — that was called the dash, you know — an' in ten minutes the butter was there.

'The priest said to her, "Your butter, ma'am, was goin' south." She knew then who was workin' the piseógs. That was the priest's way of lettin' her know that 'twas this woman that was doin' it without mentionin' any name.'

'Here's another one I heard about the workin' of piseógs. There was an old woman — I have her name but there's no need to mention it — an' she was steeped in piseógs. She could nearly take the cream out o' the milk, after you milkin it out o' the cow, without a separator or anything like that. But, one o' the neighbouring women had in her kitchen window a lovely ivy-leaf geranium in a box. An' one day this old woman went in to her. 'Twould be about the month o' June, an' the geranium was trained all around the window. An' 'twas full of lovely pink flowers.

'But when this old woman went in to her she asked her to give her a slip o' the geranium, an' she gladly gave it to her. The old woman brought home the slip an' she sowed it in a box in the kitchen window. The next thing was, it started to grow, an' grow, an' grow. An' the neighbour's geranium started to wither, an' wither, an' wither. An' the next thing was, the branches of the neighbour's geranium withered, an' the branches of the old woman's geranium grew around the kitchen. An' the next thing was, the old woman's geranium, there was a lovely coat of flowers on it, an' the neighbour's geranium, 'twas like a bit of a pencil that was stuck down in the middle o' the box. An' that was that.'

'I heard another one about that old woman too. There were two brothers an' a sister in Quin — I knew 'em well — an' they had a bit o' land. The first field was a crag an' the second field was level, an' they used to have this level field tilled, a garden in it. And, when they'd be dig- gin' the potatoes, there was several years that the potatoes used to be only something bigger than marbles. So, the rumour went around, anyway, about this old woman workin' the piseógs May Eve; that was the thirtieth of April.

'But this May Eve, anyway, I s'pose about ten o' clock, one o' the brothers, he went down to the garden. An' in the wall between the garden an' the next field there was a white-thorn hedge with a big white-thorn bushes growin' in it, an' the branches of these bushes, they were hangin' down to the ground at the two sides o' the wall. An' in the summer time if there were cattle in the next field they'd go in under the branches from the sun.

'Anyway, this man went down about ten or eleven o' clock on the thirtieth of April. He went in under the branches of these white-thorns an' he waited to see was there any piseógs or anything like that going to be done. He was there about an hour when in through a stile that was below near a drain came the old woman an' she havin' an apron on her, an' she had the apron gathered up in the bottom in one of her hands. But, she went up the garden o' potatoes, anyway, an' she stooped down in several places an' she rooted the earth with her hand an' went away somewhere else an' did the same thing. In several places she did this, an' then she went away again an' went out the stile again below at the trench. When she went out the stile my man came out from under the bush an' he went around to a few places where she went, an' he saw where the earth was rooted. So he searched it an' when he rooted the earth again what did he get in it but empty eggshells. So that was proof that she was workin' the piseógs.

'She was takin' their spuds for three or four years an' for that three of four years when these brothers used to be diggin, all they used to get in the garden was somethin' like big marbles. An' the old woman had about a half an acre o' potatoes, an' in that half an acre she had as much potatoes as that these brothers hadn't in one

acre, or an acre an' a half. So that was more proof of her
piseógs.'

'Did you know this, Eddie, that I'm able to divine. I
have hundreds o' springs found. But I'll only guarantee
to get water up to a depth of about forty feet. I wouldn't
chance it any more than that. Now, suppose you asked
me to get a spring for you, an' you say, "There! Try that
place," I get a fork of a fruit-bearing branch, white-thorn
now, or hazel or apple. An' d'you know what'll work for
me too? An osier. Well now, you tell me to try that
place. I walk around. Now, when I'm approaching a
spring, if 'tis within forty feet I'll find the pull on the
gabhlóg, on the fork in my hand. The nearer I'm coming
to it, then, the stronger the pull is gettin' an' when I
come directly over it if I thought to hold it, if I thought to
hold the gabhlóg, the skin'd come off it in my hands, or
else 'twould break, if I thought to hold it.

'Anyway, it turns downwards. Well, let me pass out
that spring then an' it starts to rise instead o' goin' downwards. Now, it goes down in a certain place. You want
to find out then what depth that spring is. Well, where it
goes down from me I mark it with the heel o' my boot.
Now I go away at some side of the mark an' I hold the
fork in the same position again, an' if I'm down on the
spring, where I go, 'twill turn downwards. If I'm not I'll
turn around slowly an' when the spring is behind me the
fork'll come up to me, turn up.

'Now, if it turns up I'll go back until I come directly
over it, until it goes down again, an' mark it there again.
From the first mark I made to that mark is the direction
'tis going. Now I stand over it, walk slowly at right
angles from it until the pull leaves the fork. I won't be
accurate but that's about the depth 'tis down. I could be
gone twenty feet from it but that doesn't say that 'tis
twenty feet deep. I found out by experience that I could

be out about two feet. An' sometimes I'd hit it accurate, d'you know what I mean. If I said 'twas twenty feet it could be eighteen, or twenty-two.

'No! A river or a drain is no good. The only water I can find is what's under the ground. An' some people, they ask me to know would an ash plant work, or an elm branch. I tried it. No! They wouldn't stir. I can't explain it.'

'How did I begin water divining? Well, I'll tell you now. The first Sunday o' June, 1946 I was at Grady's house in Kilmurry, an' while we were eatin' the dinner who came in only Jack Liddy from Ballycar. An' when he came in, "Bedad, Jack," sez Jack Grady to him, "you came."

'"I did," sez he. "I never refused anyone."

'He was tellin' me then why he came.

'"Begod," sez he, "there durin' the week Jack Grady was askin' me to know would I look for a spring for him, an' I told him I would. So I told him I'd come over today an' here I am," sez he, "came."

'So he drank a cup o' tea an' after we all went out. An' he went across the road into a bog, an' he cut two forks of a black sally in the bog. He came back, an' Jack Grady an' I, we were standin' about half way between the house an' the road.

'"Where do you want to get it, Jack?" sez he to Jack Grady.

'"Try around the house there," sez Jack to him.

'He tried the front o' the house. No good. Well, he went out, anyway, in a little garden that was at the end of it. He tried around it. He went over as far as a bit o' cabbage that Jack Grady had sown. No stir. He came back again an' into the yard at the back o' the house. There was a little gate goin' out o' the yard into a field — I suppose there'd be no more than about an acre an' a half in it. An' he was gone, I s'pose, about twenty yards from the gate, an' I was walkin' behind him, I was kind o' walkin' sideways from him, when I saw the fork turnin' down in his hand.

'"Bedad," sez he, "we struck oil. There's something here."

'It pointed straight down to the ground, an', "Hold on," sez he, "now, 'till I try which way is it goin'."

'So he marked it with the heel of his boot, an' he went down kind of angle-wise towards the road, about four or five yards. Then he caught the *gabhlóg* again in the way that he caught it first, an' it started to turn up to him.

'"Bedad," sez he, "'tis behind me."

'He only went back two or three yards when down it went again.

'"That spring," sez he, "is crossing the road."

'"Show it to me, Jack," sez I to him, "until I try will I get it."

'"Here," sez he to me. "There's the *gabhlóg* for you."

'I took the fork anyway, an' where Jack Liddy was standin' I held it in the same way as he held it.

'"Squeeze it now," sez Jack, "an' don't let it turn."

'Now, when I found it goin' I squeezed my fingers on it, an' the more I was squeezin' my fingers on it the more 'twas goin'. It kind o' frightened me. Didn't I throw it out o' my hand.

'"Name o' God," sez Jack Liddy to me. "'tis only a bit of a stick. 'Twon't bite you. Pick it up again," sez he, "an' hold it."

'I picked it up again an' the same thing, it started to go. When it started to go, "Walk out a yard or two now from it," sez Jack Liddy. I did. It started to turn up.

'"You know what," sez he to me, "you're as good as myself at it. Now, you want to find out," sez he, "what depth that is. Well, we know which way 'tis goin'. 'Tis comin' down there," sez he, "from the hill, an' 'tis goin' out across the road, an' maybe," sez he, "into the lake. But," sez he, "now, I'll show you."

'He stood over it with the other fork, an' he held it level. He walked out from it, very slowly. It started to turn up this way, now, an' when 'twas up straight it stopped that way.

'"Now," sez he, "measure that from where I am to where the mark is."

'He made three yards of it, three steps.

'"Now 'tis roughly," sez he, "about ten feet there."

'"D'you know what?" sez Jack Grady to him. "There's an oul' blind drain, now, at the other side o' the road, an' 'tis two or three feet lower than that, an' maybe more, an' I might get it," sez he, "below in the drain an' it'll take a few feet off o' me in the sinkin' of it."

'I went out in the road, an' Jack Liddy went out, an' I had the other fork o' the oul' black sally. So I walked over the road an' down it went opposite where he got it in the field.

'"Hold on," sez Jack to me, "till I see are you accurate, or are you any way near it."

'He came over the very same place. But, anyway, Eddie, I went down the drain then, down in the dry drain, an' got it again. An' Jack Liddy got it in the drain again too.

'"You'll get it there," sez Jack, "at six feet. You'll get it in the drain." But, himself an' Jack Grady, they dug it. An' at eight feet they got it in the drain. An' 'twould supply County Clare, what they got.'

'I didn't know that I was able to divine until that. But, out o' that I started on my own an' people were pullin' me an' draggin' me here an' there to look for this spring an' that spring for 'em. An' God knows, d'you know, 'tisn't much I ever made out of it.'

'Now, below in Dromullen there was a division of an outside farm of the Butlers of Castlecrin, an' the Land Commission divided it. Down near Butler's lake now, from the lake, there was a formation. I s'pose 'twould be seven or eight yards wide, an' 'twas around in a semi-circle, I could say, of low ground with bull-rushes grow-ing in it. Well now, inside in that 'twas high an' green with the formation of a lot of small little buildings in it. The place was known as Castle Island.

'But, 'twas rumoured that there was gold buried there. So, one evening the County Council workers, they were cleanin' a trench from Butler's lake up to a main trench that was from the Tírín lake into Fay's lake. I went in to 'em an' I was tellin' 'em about Castle Island, that there was supposed to be gold buried there. Now, Jack Liddy from Ballycar — the man I was tellin' you about a while ago — he was a foreman with the Council, an' also an old water diviner, an' he said that any mineral, whether 'twas gold or iron, or whatever 'twas, 'twould respond to a divining rod.

'So, after they finishin' work Jack Liddy an' I, we went in to this Castle Island. Jack cut a fork of a black sally goin' in. 'Twas growin' in the wall. We went in, anyway, an' Jack had this fork o' the black sally an' I had a shovel. An' I can imagine I see him now, goin' up along the foundation of a wall of the biggest building that was in it. An' above near the end of it the rod went down from him, in his hands, with a vengeance.

'"'Pon my word," sez he, "there's something here. Show me that shovel," sez he to me. I gave him the shovel an' he started diggin', rootin'. Next thing he got was loose stones an' lime mortar. He rooted up the stones, anyway, an' he went down about a foot an' a half in it, or two feet. He got the divining rod again an' he held it over it. It went down from him.

'"I'll root another bit," sez he.

'He rooted away, anyway, an' he wasn't gone down six inches when 'tis the very same as a big lump o' coal that he shovelled up out of it. I brought it away about seven or eight yards from where he was diggin'. He got the divining rod again an' he tried it. No stir. He went over to this oul' lump of what he thought was coal, an' it took the rod from him, whatever it was.

'But anyway, the followin' Sunday didn't I go in an' I broke a bit of it with a hammer, an' I sent it to the Department of Industry and Commerce to know what it was. An' they sent me back a letter telling me that it was a mineral known as chert.

'So, in a few Sundays after didn't Johnny McInerney, who was a friend o' mine, an' I, we went in with a shovel rootin' around, an' a divining rod, a fork of a black sally. So, in a small little building that was at the southern end of it the divining rod went down with a vengeance from me, so I started rootin'. An' I went down about two feet through loose stones an' oul' mortar, an' I came down to a flag, an' just on top o' the flag where I was rootin' there'd be about four pound of copper nails. I took 'em up out of it an' Johnny McInerney took 'em. I s'pose they'd be about six or eight inches long, square nails, an' they pure copper. But, sure, they were no good.

'Well now, Dromullen, the name suggests 'twas from the old Irish "Drom Muilinn", which means in English "the Back of the Mill". Well, could it be possible 'twould be some sort of a mill that was there one time?'

3. The Lure of Buried Treasure

'I was tellin' you, now, wasn't I, about the gold that was found below at Moohaun? Well, let me tell you that there's plenty more that's buried too, but 'twas never got. An' I know about one bit of it. I'll tell you, now.

'Richard de Clare, he was a Norman that owned Bunratty an', I s'pose, all the demesne around it. But, a grandson o' Brian Boru's — that'd be Donncha O'Brien — he attacked him in Bunratty an' defeated him. But de Clare, according to what I heard, had gold ware, cups an' saucers an' mugs an' jugs an' dishes an' all the rest of it. They were all gold. Now, de Clare also had a castle in Feenish, an' didn't he collect all the gold ware he had in Bunratty an' hit for the castle in Feenish. I suppose that'd be about six miles in a boat, an' to go across the country, I suppose 'twould be three or four, anyway.

'But, in a few months didn't Donncha O'Brien attack him again in Feenish, an' defeated him there again. Rather than let O'Brien an' his army have the gold ware de Clare put 'em all into a boat an' brought 'em out in the Shannon, an' he sank the boat, ware an' all, an' went down with the boat himself.

'Now, years ago didn't divers come from Dublin to go down to look for this treasure, but there was some sort of a serpent below around the boat that attacked 'em when they went down, an' they couldn't go near the boat. But, where the boat went down there's a whirlpool over it an' 'tis known as the Boordig Flood. An' if you were out in the Shannon around the island, fishing, you'd want to be more than careful in a boat because the whirlpool would suck you into it.

'An' the ruins o' the castle are still there in Feenish. There's a hill there too, away a bit from the castle an' if you went up on the hill after dark you'd see a light in a window that's in the castle. After dark, now! An' when you'd see the light, if you went down towards it there'd be no light there when you'd get down. An' I don't think 'tis the reflection of the moon, because there's no glass or nothing in the windows.'

'There was an old man living by himself at Ballykilty, an' to go to his house you'd pass down at the back of Quin school, down a place they call Ryne. Below Ryne was the townland of Ballykilty, an' you pass down Ballykilty on the road to Moohaun. There was a road, then, turning to the right just below Ballykilty wood, an' that was a continuation, I'd say, of the old road that was made in Brian Boru's time. 'Twas going on to Ard Solas, that old road. But 'twas on that old road that this old man lived.

'But, this fellow I knew well now, we'll call him Tom, he was workin' with a local farmer an' maybe three or four nights in the week he'd go to this old man, you see, to keep him company. Anyway, 'twould be after Christmas one year, in January, that Tom went to the old man and this night he was tellin' him that there was a ruin of an old house about seventy or eighty yards from the fort that was in his field. An' Tom knew the field as well as he knew his left hand; 'twas across the road from the gate of the farmer he was workin' for. I s'pose there'd be about ten or twelve acres in the field, an' 'twas at the far side o' the field from the road the fort was. Now, about seventy or eighty yards from the fort there was a ruin of an old house, an' the old man told him that there was supposed to be gold buried under the flag of the entrance door to this old house, but a life would have to be lost in the getting of it. 'Twould be got alright but there would have to be a life lost in the getting of it. Anyway, Tom said no more, but the followin' day he was tellin' some o' the boys around Quin about what the old man was tellin' him about the gold being buried under the flag o' the door of this ruin of the old house. But anyway, Tom, one evenin' that he was goin' home he went to inspect it an' outside the door, the entrance door o' the old house, there was a heap o' stones, and, coverin' these stones there was moss an' grass.

'Now, to describe the house to you. An' I saw the house! 'Twas down to the tops o' the windows. The formations of the windows were there but the top lintels were gone off of 'em, you see. One gable end of the house was standin' an' the other was knocked. An' I s'pose 'twould be about forty yards at the Moohaun side of the oul' house this old man, he had a galvanised shed made for calves there, an' he had a door in the house an' all.

'But at the back, then, o' the ruin o' the oul' house there was what I could call a haggart where, I suppose, the occupants, they had a garden. This was enclosed by another wall. Well, from the end of the ruin o' the oul' house up to the old man's house that he had made for the calves, there was a double wall; 'twas built with dry stones, an' there'd be rough stones on top of it.

'Anyway when Tom told the boys around Quin about the yarn that the old man told him about the gold bein' buried they made up a plan, that some night they'd go to dig for it. An' they'd have to wait, o' course, until everyone was in bed, the old man in particular. 'Twas on his land, you see. But they agreed, anyway, to go of a moonlight night in June or July that year.

'So, they waited until the month o' July, of one night that there was a full moon, an' Tom, Christy, Joe, Martin an' another John — we'll leave their family names out of it 'cos some of 'em are still alive — they went an' they armed with pickaxes an' shovels. An' Martin, he brought a bottle o' holy water in case of any

evil spirits. But anyway, they went at about eleven o'
clock or half eleven, when they thought that everyone
was in bed, you see. An' they went to this old house an'
they started rootin'. They rooted down, rooted the heap
o' stones that was in the front o' the entrance door, an'
what was mixed with the heap o' stones, Tom told me,
was old lime mortar, an' the stones weren't very big.'

'Anyway, they went down about four feet an' John —
he's alive yet — he went down in the hole, throwin' up
loose stones out of it, an' oul' lime mortar, with a
shovel. The next thing he came across was a flag, an' he
sez to 'em, "Bedad boys we have it."

'The flag was bigger than the hole that they had made
so he started rootin' down one side o' the hole to make it
wider, d'you see, so that he'd come to the edge o' the
flag. While he was rootin' down one side o' the hole
what came along the top o' the wall from the old man's
house only what they thought was a white cat. An' he
jumped up on the wall o' the ruin o' the old house an'
jumped across the formation o' the windows until he
came between the first window from the door an' the
second window. He sat there above on top o' the wall
an' he started spittin' at 'em, Tom told me. A cat spittin', now, did you ever hear him? 'Tssshhh! 'Tssshhh!
'Tssshhh! An' every spit that he'd give, Tom told me the
sparks o' fire used to come out of his mouth. An' didn't
the boys start peltin' him with stones. An' he jumped
across the window again an' ran along the top o' the
double stone wall that the old man, I s'pose, built. He
went up on the galvanised o' the house that the old man
had for the calves an' sat above on the galvanised about
forty yards away from 'em, an' he spittin'. An' the boys
started peltin' him with stones again so he went up the
roof o' the house an' down the other side an' they saw no
more of him.

'But John, anyway, he was below in the hole an' he

throwin' up the loose stones out of it, an' the mortar, an' he came to the side o' the flag, Eddie. There was a hole down an' a stone fell down, an' fell down the hole. Now, surely to goodness, Tom told me, that from once the stone fell down until it reached the bottom it took about a minute to fall. 'Twas unknown the depth of it!

'John, anyway, he said that they'd get up the flag whatever depth it was. So he started at the other side o' the hole an' as soon as he started at that side, in from the fort came what they though was a sheep. An' the sheep came slowly in from the fort, an' when 'twas about half-way between the fort an' the hole they were openin' the sheep took a jump an' landed into the hole by the side of John. John, he was pitched, I s'pose, about forty yards away with the shovel in his hand, whatever it was that put him out of the hole an' flyin' though the air. They all ran, out to the road, an' left shovels an' hacks an' all after 'em. 'Twas Martin that had the bottle o' holy water but 'twas Christy that got the contents o' the bottle goin' out the field. When they went out on the road they didn't know what to do. When the old man would come next day an' see the hole open an' the heap o' stones up out of it there'd be holy murder. But, John agreed to go back an' close the hole some hour o' the mornin', I s'pose it might be three or four o' clock in the mornin', for fear the old man might see it. So he did; he went back an' he brought a crowbar an' three shovels an' a pickaxe out with him. He left 'em at a house in Quin until they'd give 'em back to the owners.'

'Another place they thought to find something was at Quin Abbey. O, they did. Now, under Quin Abbey there's supposed to be a cellar, and, in the cellar the ware of the abbey is supposed to be, cups an' saucers an' mugs an' jugs an' teapots, an' unknown what. 'Tis unknown, I s'pose, what they'd be worth now.

'But didn't some o' the boys, they thought to look for 'em one night. At the back o' the abbey, now, facing Daingean Breac castle, there's an arch. You can see it plain. Well, at the outer portion of the arch there's a building, a square building. Up about the height of an ordinary man's chest, under the arch, there's a window, an' you can look down an' I s'pose 'twould be ten or twelve feet down to the bottom. Now, below, if you look down the window, you can see the formation of a door below at the bottom, an' above on top then 'tis the sky you'll see when you look up. You can get at this building from above too. If you go up the stairs when you go in the entrance gate o' the abbey you'll go up to a green patch. Continue on over straight, an' there's a drop down then, beyond, down in this square building, an' a couple of iron bars goin' across.

'But, what did they do, these three fellows? They thought the formation o' the door below, you see, was the entrance to the cellar, an' they brought in a ladder one night, an' a crowbar, when all the boys in Quin were in bed, an' the girls as well. They brought up the ladder up the stairs, anyway, an' they put it down from the green patch, down to the bottom. One of 'em went down with his crowbar an' he took two or three stones out o' the top o' this entrance door. An' whatever look he gave wasn't there a friar standing by the side of him. He left the crowbar there. He told me he didn't know how he went up the ladder. An' himself an' another one of 'em, they pulled up the ladder an' off with 'em as fast as ever they could. I can tell you they went out of the abbey a lot faster than they came in. An' that finished 'em with the cellar an' the ware. But later on they had to come back again, bring ladder an' all, put it down again an' bring up the crowbar for fear anyone might see it below an' know what was being done. I don't know which of 'em went down for it, though. I'd say it wasn't

the man that saw the friar. If 'twas myself that was in it
I'd leave the oul' crowbar there to the devil.

'But I must tell you more about that abbey, 'cos tis a
very interesting place, most interesting.'

4. Hallowed Places.

'Quin Abbey, now; did you ever hear about the founding of that abbey? 'Twas built, in 1402 I think, by John MacNamara of Daingean.

'Well, now, these stories about the founding of it you can judge for yourself. The truth of one of 'em seems to be more authentic than the other one, but you can judge for yourself.

'The first story is that he had one son whom he called Síoda MacNamara. An' one mornin' he was missing. They were livin' in Daingean, o' course; that'd be, I s'pose, about three an' a half miles or four from Quin. They searched everywhere for him. Couldn't find him. They searched next day, an' the third day they found him in a pond that was near the castle. I know, now, where the oul' formation o' the pond is. 'Tisn't a dozen yards from the castle. This oul' pond, now, last time I saw it, 'twas dry but 'twould take in an area of about roughly half an acre. An' 'twas all rough oul' ground, you know, an' lumps here an' there in it. On these lumps there were bull-rushes growin' an' 'twould give you the idea that at one time 'twas full o' water.

'But, anyway, the third day that Síoda was missin' their neighbours, I s'pose, or his father, got him in the pond, drowned. He brought him into the castle. He there an' then took an oath to the Almighty God that if he was restored to life he'd build a monastery for the Franciscan friars at Quin. The followin' feast of Saint Francis, Síoda was playin' an' friskin' around the castle again!

'John MacNamara gathered a crowd of neighbours an' masons an' they started the abbey in Quin on the ruins of an old Norman castle that was there. There were four round towers in it. He constructed the abbey, an' the abbey was to be, according to the way I heard it, a thousand paces long, an' five hundred paces wide. So there's only, I suppose, an eighth of it there now.

'But at the back of the present parish church in Quin that's in Bobby Clune's field in Daingean Breac you can see the formation of the walls in the field. If you went up the tower in Quin Abbey, now — the tower is exactly a hundred feet high — an' looked towards John Clune's, you'd see all the formation of the houses. The river wasn't where it is now at all then, an' the abbey was goin' right up as far as the present street.

'Now, I gave a hand at the building of Saint Finian's Hall in Quin, an' Canon Vaughan, he bought Dan Clune's house — 'twas a thatched house — an' the garden at the back of it. So, they knocked the house, an' in the sinkin' o' the foundation they went down twelve feet in it, an' the twelve feet they got were, eight feet o' the finest o' grey sand an' four feet of earth on top of it. They kept that sand to make concrete blocks out of it. They got as far as rock then an' they filled with stones — they got 'em in the bank o' the river above the abbey. But, through the sand an' through the earth there were eight horse-loads o' bones got in it, an' skulls. So they came to the conclusion that there should have been a battle fought there one time, when all the bones an' skulls were there. An' there was, too.

'Well, the other story that's told about it was this, an' all I can say, now, are the words o' the man that told it to me. There was a holy man at Tom Fionnlach, an' John MacNamara of Daingean had several dreams an' in these dreams he saw friars wandering about looking for a home an' a place to teach. But he went to this holy man, anyway, to know what his dreams were about. But, the holy man said to him, according to what I was told, "Now, the Franciscan friars; you had dreams about 'em. Well, in fact," sez the holy man, "I had dreams too about these Franciscan friars, that they wanted a home an' a school. Is it possible for you to build one?"

'"Well," sez John Mac to him, "my son is after bein' got in a pond, unconscious, an' I'll do anything," sez he, "that my son will live."

'"Is it possible for you," sez the holy man to him, "to build an abbey or a monastery for these holy friars?"

'"Money is no object to me," sez John Mac to him. "Will I build here?"

'"No," sez the holy man. "You'll build at the village of your own parish. Part o' the foundation is laid for you in an old Norman castle. You'll build there."

'He started the abbey, an' as soon as he did his son was as well as ever he was.

'So they're the two stories that were told about the founding of Quin Abbey.'

'According to old local people the abbey was commenced in 1402. I told you that already. But according to Tommy Mac in Crevagh it took thirty years to build it, and, at the opening ceremony that John MacNamara who was responsible for the commencing of it was there, an' his son was there, Francis Síoda MacNamara, an' a man whose name was John Clune. This John Clune, in his youth, he got infantile paralysis an' lost the use of his two legs, an' he used to go about on his hands an' knees. Anyway, at the opening ceremony the friars had him there, an' John Mac's son had him there. An' according to Tommy Mac — who claimed that he was a descendant of John Mac that founded the abbey — when they opened it John Mac was ninety-four years of age. An' according to Tommy Mac the friars prayed over John Clune who was goin' around on his hands an' knees, an' after some prayers he stood up an' walked about. An' the friars said that as long as the parish o' Quin would be the parish o' Quin 'twould never be without a Mac-Namara or a Clune family. An' 'tis full o' MacNamaras an' Clunes today.'

'When the friars were in the abbey there was a bakery in Quin; 'twas opposite the church. An' the bakery was owned by Denis Moloney. Well, at the right-hand side of the house where he lived there was a one-storey house — 'twas attached on to it — an' that was the bake-house that Denis Moloney had. But when the friars were in the abbey they went short o' bread one day an' two of 'em, they went out to the bakery, an' Denis Moloney an' his baker were inside. One of 'em went to the door an' he says that they were short o' bread in the abbey, would they give him bread.

'"I will," sez Denis Moloney, "if you have the money for it."

'"Oh," sez the friar, "our rule is that we're not allowed to handle any money whatsoever. But," sez he, "if you'll give us the bread you'll be rewarded."

'"An' who's goin' to reward me?" sez Denis Moloney.

'"The Almighty," sez the friar to him.

'"Go 'way," sez Denis Moloney.

'So the friar walked away. He went out to the other man an' he told him. "Go back," sez the other man, "an' tell him that the oven o' bread that he has down bakin' will be the last oven of yeast bread that will ever be made in Quin."

'So he went back an' told Denis Moloney, "That oven o' bread," sez he, "that you have down bakin' will be the last oven of yeast bread that'll ever be made in Quin."

'He walked away from the door after sayin' that, an' walked out to the other friar that was outside in the street. One of 'em went down Ballymaclune an' the other went down Moohaun, lookin' for bread. The people of Ballymaclune an' the people of Moohaun, not alone did they give 'em bread but they gave 'em every kind of vegetables; onions, cabbage, parsnips, carrots, potatoes; meat, bacon, they even gave 'em. They brought it up to the abbey to 'em in horses an' cars according to the story I heard. An' the friars said that the people of the two townlands would never be short of anything as long as they'd live, or their families wouldn't. And, the people of Ballymaclune an' Moohaun are some o' the best off people in the parish o' Quin to this day.

'But, the dozen o' bread that Denis Moloney had down, when he thought it was baked he opened the oven an' pulled out the trays. Every loaf of it was as big as four loaves. He was delighted. Himself an' his baker, they filled the tins again, put 'em into the oven an' left 'em whatever length o' time it takes to bake, whether 'tis an hour or an hour an' a half. But when he opened the oven for his bread 'twas the very same as he put it in, only turned a brown colour. It never rose. He closed the oven door again on it, left it so for another hour an' a half. When he opened it after the three hours 'tis a sledge you'd want to break it. He put down another round of it an' 'twas the same thing. Denis Moloney had to give up the bakery.

'Years after, a woman, she started a bakery in Quin, years after the friars were all dead an' gone out o' the abbey. 'Twas the very self an' same way with her. 'Twould never rise. The yeast bread'll never rise in Quin. An' there's no bakery there to this day.

'But the abbey isn't the only interesting thing in Quin. There's a blessed well there an' I'd say the like of it isn't in Ireland.

'You see, Saint Finian was the patron saint of Quin, an' there was a blessed well dedicated to him there. An' I'll tell you now where that blessed well is. You know where Saint Finian's Hall is built — the one I was tellin' you I was in the buildin' of it? Well, when you face in the hall turn to your left-hand side, an' go down by the side o' the hall, down to the far end of it. And, there's a double stone wall built between Dan Clune's garden and the Protestant church, an' at the hall side o' the Protestant church, below at the far end of it, you'll see a hollow in the ground with a sort of a curved stone. 'Tis a natural rock that was at the back of it, an' there's a hollow in the front o' the rock, an' 'twas there the blessed well was supposed to be one time.

'But at the time of Queen Elizabeth, her army and horse soldiers invaded Quin. And, they brought a horse to the blessed well to give him a drink. An' the horse was thirsty o' course an' he stooped down to the blessed well — there was no protection whatsoever to the blessed well. The horse stooped down, drinkin' the water out o' the well, an' the next thing was, the horse lay down on the ground an' died.

'So they pulled in another horse, an' the same thing happened; the second horse died. An' they brought in the third one an' the third died. They brought in the fourth one . . . when the well went dry! An' where the blessed well came up again was up in the fork of an ash tree that was between the abbey an' John Clune's house in Quin. You can't miss it. If you go down at the back o' the present church there's a wall between that an' another field, an' there's only the one tree in it, a big ash tree.

'Now, there are two branches in the tree growing out over the oul' wall, an' there's a lump on the tree, an' if you g'up on the wall an' step up on the lump an' catch one o' the branches you can pull yourself up, an' you'll see down at the fork o' the branches a hole. An' the hole is full o' water. An' left in the wall an' around the butt o' the tree are scraps of rosary beads an' medals. Even in the summer time the water is runnin' down along the tree, an' it has nowhere to go only around the butt o' the tree. I went in to see it myself one time. I got up on the tree an' saw it. The hole is there. You could put about a tea-cup into it, an' 'tis full o' water.

'But I wonder, Eddie — although I wouldn't touch it myself — I wonder if the tree was cut would the well be got? An' wouldn't you think the water constantly flowing would rot the tree? But no! 'Tis there as sound as ever.'

'I'll bet you never heard the story of Fenloe blessed well! I heard it from an old man below in Fenloe the best part o' forty years ago an' why I remember it so clearly is because I had trial of that well myself. You could say I'm a believer in it.

'In the present parish of Newmarket-on-Fergus in olden times there were seven parishes. I might be wrong in the first three of them, the parish of Careera, the parish of Kilconry an' the parish of Kilmoleary, but I'm not wrong in the parish of Fenloe. That name was shortened to Fenloe from the old name Tom Fionnlach. Tom Fionnlach, or Fenloe as it is now shortened, was on the road from Newmarket-on-Fergus to Kilkishen. It's now a townland, an' when you leave Newmarket to go to this townland you can go by Ballycar, an' the next townland to Ballycar is Fenloe.

'This was one time a parish as I have already mentioned. There's a blessed well there by the roadside, and many years I've seen people doing rounds at that blessed well. An' what they were doing for their rounds was just simply walking around the blessed well with rosary beads in their hands sayin' the rosary. I heard people say that there were special rounds to be done at the well but I didn't know how to do 'em. People used to tell me about these rounds but they didn't know exactly what they were.

'Now, there was a man from Knappogue, Jimmy Moloney was his name, an' I asked him did he know the special rounds that were to be done at Fenloe blessed well. He told me to go to Michael Conlon in Fenloe — that's the old man I told you about — that he knew the rounds.

'So one evening I went over to Michael an' I asked him what were the special rounds that were to be done at the blessed well. He said to me that I would want to know the story of the blessed well to do the special rounds, an' he told me the story, an' this is it.

'About a hundred years after the time Saint Patrick was in Ireland there was a small college at Fenloe where a few priests used to be educated, and over this small college there was a priest appointed whose name was Father Lucticern. Now, at this time there was a disease very prevalent in Ireland which was cholera, an' many people suffered with this disease. Michael Conlon told me that the disease used to appear in the form of a lump or lumps on the head which were very painful.

'Attached to the small little college there was some land, an' the students there, they used have a garden an' hay an' cows, an' maybe cattle. One day, in the summer time they were out in the fields saving hay, this Father Lucticern an' some of his boys when they heard a woman screaming, "I have the cholera! I have the cholera!"

'Father Lucticern called her an' asked her to come over to him. She went over to him and he put up his hand where there was a big lump in the side of her head an' he took the lump an' hit it against a rock that was in the field. He called one of his boys an' asked him what he thought of what he did, an' the first fellow he called only laughed at him an' said 'twas only foolishness an' codology. Father Lucticern, he called a second fellow an' he asked him.

"'Well," sez he, "I kind o' believe," sez he, "that 'tis a miracle from God."

"'You only kind o' believe it?" sez Father Lucticern to him.

"'That's all," sez he.

"'Stand back there, my good man," sez he, the same as he did to the first fellow. He called the third fellow an' asked him.

"'Well, Father," sez he, "I firmly believe that 'tis a miracle from God worked through you, Father."

"'You firmly believe it?" sez Father Lucticern to him.

"'I do," sez the third fellow.

"'Well," sez he. "d'you see those three smaller stones there in the field? In the morning," sez he, "the image of your countenance will appear on these three stones. You," sez he, "that laughed at me and scorned when I asked you what you thought I did, the image of your countenance will not be visible in that stone. Your face will appear there all right, but your eyes, nose an' mouth will not be visible.

"'You," sez he, "that partly believed, or kind o' believed in me, your face will appear there," sez he, "but the images of your eyes, nose an' mouth will only be partly visible on that stone."

"'You," sez he, "that thoroughly an' firmly believed in me, the image of your countenance will appear on that stone as plain as you have your features now, an' that stone," sez he, "where I stuck the cholera to will remain there, an' this story will be told about me as long as the parish of Tom Fionnlach is the parish of Tom Fionnlach, an' the disease of the cholera will not prevail within two miles radius of that rock," sez he, "where I stuck it."

"'Now," sez Michael Conlon to me, "that's the story of Fenloe, or in former years as it was known, Tom Fionnlach. Right! You want to do the special rounds at

Fenloe blessed well. Here they are, as told to me by my father, and I suppose," sez he, "the same story was told to him by his father before him. The feast day of St Lucticern is the twenty-eight of April and at any time after twelve o' clock the night before up to twelve o' clock on the twenty-eight of April you can do the rounds at the blessed well. Now, when you go in to the blessed well don't touch the water when you go in first. Only kneel down, bless yourself, say an Our Father an' ten Hail Marys an' a Glory be to the Father. When you have the Glory be to the Father said bless yourself with the water from the well. Now, you go into the graveyard, Fenloe graveyard, an' when you go in the front gate or in the stile which is by the side o' the gate turn to your right over the graveyard, an' there's a new bit of a wall built by the county council — 'tis between the graveyard an' Fenloe kitchen garden — an' up on that wall the three heads are. The three heads, before that, they were in the graveyard wall that's around the graveyard, but where they were the wall fell an' the three heads were scattered. But, the County Council renovated the graveyard, an' they built a new bit of a wall, which was also knocked, probably by a storm, between the graveyard an' Fenloe kitchen garden. Well, when they were building the new wall they brought the three heads an' they built 'em into the new wall between the graveyard an' the kitchen garden, an' they're still there."

"'Well, as I said, when you have your Our Father, ten Hail Marys an' Glory be to the Father said at the blessed well bless yourself with the water from the well. Then go to the three heads, kneel down, say an Our Father, three Hail Marys an' a Glory be to the Father, and after that you say 'Thanks be to God I am not like you who laughed an' scorned at Saint Lucticern when he cured the woman of the cholera. I firmly believe that through his intercession my favour or request will be granted'."

"'Now," sez Michael Conlon to me, "there's something in this. Do not go out the way you went in, not out the gate or out the stile you came in, but cross the graveyard, and opposite Jute's vault there's a stile in the wall. There are three stones inside an' three more outside, sticking out o' the wall, an' you go up those stones an' down the other side outside. When you go down outside go down straight to the corner and the cholera stone is at the ground level just at the corner. You can't miss it 'cos there's a big lump in the middle of it. And when you get there kneel down, say an Our Father, three Hail Marys and a Glory be to the Father, and when you say Glory be to the Father there an' kiss the stone your first round is done."

"'Go to the blessed well again, kneel down, say your Our Father, ten Hail Marys, Glory be to the Father, bless yourself with the water, then go to the three heads again, kneel down, say an Our Father, three Hail Marys an' a Glory be to the Father, an' after that you say 'Thanks be to God I am not like you who partly believed in Saint Lucticern. I firmly believe that through his intercession my favour or request will be granted.' Then you cross the graveyard the same as you did the first time, out the stile opposite Jute's vault, down to the corner to the cholera stone, kneel down again, say your Our Father, three Hail Marys an' a Glory be to the Father, kiss the stone. Your second round is done."

"'Go then to the blessed well, say your Our Father, ten Hail Marys an' a Glory be to the Father. Bless yourself with the water, go again to the three heads. When you go to the three heads the third time you say an Our Father, three Hail Marys an' a Glory be to the Father. After that you say 'Thanks be to God I am like you who thoroughly an' firmly believed in Saint Lucticern when he cured the woman of the cholera. I do firmly believe

that through him my favour or request will be granted.'
You cross the graveyard again, out the stile, down to the
cholera stone, say an Our Father, three Hail Marys an' a
Glory be to the Father at the cholera stone, kiss the
stone, and your three rounds are done."

'Michael Conlon also told me that when Father Lucticern blessed the well that was for the use of this small
school, he blessed it for the cure of the cholera an' after
that the people came and brought the water out of it in
bucketfuls an' barrelfuls with the result that the well
used to go down an' dry. So, for the cure of the cholera
he blessed half Fenloe lake, an' Fenloe lake is a fairly
big lake. The side of the lake next to the road is wide an'
there's a tail of water going back out o' the lake, back
nearly to the railway from Ballycar railway station on to
Sixmilebridge. According to Michael Conlon Father
Lucticern did not bless the tail at all, only the front
portion o' the lake facing the road.

'Michael Conlon also said that some man from
Limerick, years after, got the cholera, an' he was on his
way to Fenloe as he had heard about it. When he came
within the two-mile radius the lump that was on his head
fell on the ground, an' he turned back completely cured.

'That story was told to me by Michael about the last
week in March, 1948, an' here now is one o' my own
experiences of the blessed well that happened about
twelve months before that.'

'At the time, now, I'm going to relate about I didn't
know the special rounds that were to be done at the
blessed well.

'At any rate, at home in my place at Ballyroughan
there was a workman from the Co. Cavan whose name
was Mike Murphy. It'd be about the middle o'
November, 1947 that Mike an' I, we went down Ballyroughan crag cutting firewood, white-thorn bushes an'

everything we met, hazels an' black-thorns, an' we had briars to clear out of our way. We levelled a big white-thorn bush an' I got a slasher to cut the light branches off of it. After that, after cutting off the light branches I got a hatchet to cut the heavy stuff.

'I was cutting a branch, anyway, an' every stroke I used to hit it used to go from the stroke an' spring back again. So, this time it sprung back wasn't there a stump of a thorn in the branch an' it stuck in my left-hand little finger. In the evening when we came up to our tea I was showin' the finger to an aunt o' mine who had been a nurse in London for thirty years. She got a needle to try an' get out the thorn, an' the thorn was gone so far in that she couldn't bring it out. She left it so.

'Next morning the finger was swelled an' 'twas very sore. In about two days after the finger turned com-pletely yellow an' 'twas as big as four fingers. That was the little finger o' my left hand.

'Now, my aunt had ordered some rose trees from Watson's Nurseries at Killiney, Dublin, and, a deal with a day later there did a postcard come from the station-master at Ballycar station that rose trees arrived at the station for my aunt. So, at dinner time she asked me to know would I go for the rose trees to Ballycar station, which I did. The means I had o' travelling was a pony an' a round trap. Now, the finger o' my left hand was yellow an' completely swollen, an' I couldn't bend it or let it touch anything for if I did the pain would actually go out through my left shoulder. I couldn't even let it touch the reins, the leather reins that I was driving the pony with.

'But anyhow, I went over to Ballycar station an' the station-master asked me to sign for the rose trees, which I did, an' got 'em. I put 'em on the trap an' sat up, drove out of the railway station an' back by Fenloe. When I was going beyond Fenloe blessed well I just thought to myself that the well was the cure of my finger. So I pulled up at the stile going into the blessed well. I went in the stile an' I knew nothing about the special rounds that were to be done at the blessed well. But at any rate, when I went in I knelt down, blessed myself with water, said an Our Father an' three Hail Marys an' a Glory be to the Father, an' then stuck my left hand completely into the well. When I took it out I found that the pain that was in the finger had completely left it.

'I came out over the stile, sat up on the trap, took the reins an' drove the pony over the road. I had gone, now, about a mile when I looked at the finger and the skin o' the finger was frizzled up an' no pain in it. I went home, which was about another mile, an' unharnessed the pony, let him out in the field an' threw earth on the roots of the rose trees until next day, when I sowed 'em. An' the small finger o' my left hand had reduced to its normal size.

'In about a week the skin that was frizzled on it completely peeled off an' new skin grew on it, an' my aunt or I or Mike Murphy could not understand where the thorn, the stump o' the white-thorn went.

'So I firmly recommend anybody who has a favour or a request to be granted to go to Fenloe blessed well an' do the rounds there. An' I would say that anybody who does the rounds fervently will be very rarely disappointed.'

'Talking about Fenloe graveyard reminds me of another one I heard about. You might ever hear tell of the moving graveyard. No? Well, you'll hear about it now.

'Cill Cisín means the Church of the Little Baskets. It appears that in former years there were basket-makers in Kilkishen, an' that's how it derives its name. An' probably 'twas osier woods that were growin' around it. Now, the present Kilkishen is in the parish of

O'Callaghan's Mills, but there were three divisions in the parish one time. There was O'Callaghan's Mills, Oatfield an' Kilkishen. Anyway, just outside the village there's a townland called Clonlea an' I heard that in olden times the present Kilkishen was the parish of Clonlea. An' the parish church at the time was at the top of a hill at Clonlea.

'At one time there were two priests in Kilkishen, Father Shaughnessy an' Father Tuohy. An' I'd say 'twould be about a mile an' a half or two miles in the Six-milebridge direction there was a townland called Mount Baylee an' in that townland there was a family of the Baylees who were black Protestants. In Clonlea, then, there was a family of the Moloneys. I knew that family myself. But it appears that it'd be, I suppose, a grand-father or a granduncle of the man I knew that died. Now, the parish graveyard was in Mount Baylee, on the side o' the hill. I was shown where it was. But, the Moloneys an' the Baylees, they fell out. An' they left it so. But when this Moloney died, of course the body had to be buried in Mount Baylee graveyard as it was the parish graveyard an' the family graveyard.

'The funeral proceeded from Clonlea church in a hearse an' a pair o' horses to Mount Baylee graveyard, an' when they went in the road gate they had to go up the side of a hill to the graveyard. An' when they were goin' up didn't Baylee himself come out to the four men that were carryin' the coffin. An' Baylee sez to one of 'em, "Wherever ye'll bury that fellow," sez he, "ye won't bury him in my place. Ye can throw him into the lake," sez he, "if ye like, but ye're not going to bury him in that graveyard . . . in my place."

'Father Tuohy heard him, an' he turned back — he was in front o' the coffin — an' sez to him, "Look here, Mr Baylee," sez he to him, "your house will be yet with the crows an' the jackdaws goin' in an' out through it, an' Mount Baylee will go without an heir. An' Mount Baylee," sez he, "will go without a hare. So go now, Mr Baylee, and," sez he, "you'll get a surprise very shortly. Turn back, men," sez he, "and bring that coffin, back to the church."

'They brought out the coffin again, put it into the hearse an' brought it back to the church in Clonlea. After sayin' their prayers Father Shaughnessy said to 'em, "Let ye all be here tomorrow, now, for the funeral, at the same time. An' when ye'll come tomorrow," sez he, "ye'll get a surprise."

'All went away. They congregated next day for the funeral, an' when they went into the church, to their amazement an' astonishment there were headstones an' tombstones around the church where there wasn't one the day before, an' a grave opened. They had their funeral.

'Now, the man that told me that story was Pat Hassett, an' here's how it came about. I was very fond o' fishing an' I used to go down to Pat in Cloonbrick, fishing. So, one Sunday I went down an' we did four rounds of Cloonbrick lake. 'Twas a fairly big lake, but we got nothing in it.

'"Pull out now," sez he, "out the river, out to Clonlea lake an' we'll have a great evening of it."

'I was on the oars an' out the river we went, out under the bridge in Clonlea road an' into this small little lake, as I thought.

'"In the name o' God," sez I, "this is only a pond."

'"There's pike in this," sez he, "and wait now till we go out to the big lake. If we don't get a pike in one round o' this," sez he, "there isn't a pike in Clonlea."

'One round of it, he caught one, about eight pound.

'"That fellow's brother," sez he, "is where he was. Turn in there again an' I'll get him."

'I turned in again, an' going round in the same spot he hooked another one. We got him, played him out.

"'Now," sez he, "the reeds there right opposite you, they're fairly thick. Get up a bit o' speed now an' drive the boat as far as you can through 'em."

'I knew what to do.

"'You needn't tell me at all, Pat," sez I.

'I turned out the boat an' faced straight to the reeds, an' as hard as ever I could I was pullin' on the oars. I drove the boat right in through the reeds, an' the next thing was, it stuck on the bottom. Pat had a pair o' wellingtons on him.

"'Stay in the boat now, you," sez he, "and I'll get out an' I'll pull the boat across into the big lake."

'I stood up an' I looked. I saw an odd weed growin' here an' there, an' I'd say 'twould be about forty yards farther on there was another line o' reeds. Pat pulled the boat. There wasn't four inches o' water there.

"'In the name o' goodness, Pat," sez I, "what's this? Or what sort of a place is it?"

"'That's where Clonlea graveyard crossed," he said. "That graveyard that's above around the church was beyond there," sez he, "in Mount Baylee. An' d'you see that grove o' trees beyond? Well, that's Mount Baylee. An' d'you see the hill at the left-hand side o' the row o' trees? That's where the graveyard was. I'll show it to you. I'll bring you over there someday if you come down during the week. Say, Wednesday evening the two of us can cycle over an' I'll show you," sez he, "where the graveyard left."

'I did, an' the two of us cycled over to Mount Baylee an' up the side o' the hill. An' I suppose, in all, Eddie, there'd be about three acres of a hollow in the side o' the hill, an' rabbits had burrows made in the site of it. To stand below in the centre of it, you couldn't see over the top of it. I suppose 'twould be, from the centre of it, now, up to the top, about eight feet. But 'twas saucer-shaped, you know. 'Twas goin' out shallow at the edges, an' deep in the middle. An' the rabbits had sand rooted out of it, makin' burrows, an' they rooted out bits o' bones out o' the burrows. Wouldn't that tell you that the story Pat Hassett told me could have some truth in it.'

'In that same graveyard, Clonlea graveyard, there's a light sometimes seen. I was below at Jerry Moroney's in Clonlea one night, an' Jerry lived in a cottage just below Jack Neill's forge. But the forge, d'you see, was closed for years; the forge was there but not working. Well, I was a fairly good mechanic in my time. I built bicycles, an' I used to be down at Jerry's building wheels for him.

'But this night, anyway, about half past ten, Jerry an' I came out, out to the little gate o' the cottage. We stood talkin', an' I had my back to the pier o' the gate, facing Clonlea graveyard. The next thing was, a big ball o' fire, it rose up out o' the graveyard. Now, I s'pose 'twould be about four feet in diameter. It rose up about fifteen or sixteen feet in the air an' it went slowly towards the road, towards a nearby house. An' when it came over the road it turned back in again, back into the graveyard, an' down, an' we saw no more of it.

'"Jerry," sez I, "what's that? Did you see that big ball o' fire goin' out o' the graveyard?"

'"Take no notice of that. I'll tell you now what 'tis. For three nights before a corpse goes into that graveyard that ball o' fire rises out of it an' goes out as far as the road gate an' back in again, for three nights before a body goes into it."

'An' in two days after a man died in Kilkishen, a retired postman, an' he was buried there. He was sick at the time we saw the light an' in two days after he died.

'O, 'tis strange alright, the things you could meet with.'

5. Haunted Places

'Could you believe that a heap o' stones would be haunted? I know it might seem funny but wait, now, till I explain.

'I don't know what year it was that the County Council cleaned the graveyards. Would it be 1946 or '47? Anyway, all loose stones that were in the graveyards, they paid men to collect 'em an' put 'em out on the road.

'But, below in Kilmurry graveyard, now, when you'd be takin' in a coffin you'd have to shoulder the coffin from inside the gate because the graveyard was on top of a hill. 'Twas slant-wise up the hill that you'd have to go. You'd have to turn over to your left hand an' go slant-wise, you see, up the hill for about half way to the graveyard. 'Twould be a good way beyond the graveyard when you'd have to turn again, right hand, an' go slant-wise again up to the graveyard gate. The hill was so steep that four men couldn't bring up a coffin there straight. They'd have to go slant-wise.

'Anyway, when the Council renovated the graveyards there was a ruin of a house or a church in that graveyard. I saw it myself. Part of it'd be only about two feet high, an' more of it'd be three feet or maybe more, an' 'twas inside in the graveyard. When I examined it all the wall was built with lime mortar, an 'twas all flat stones that were in it, in the wall.'

'But, the County Council workers, they collected all the stones around the graveyards, an' in Kilmurry there were tombstones, big flat stones, down on graves, an' stones under 'em. Well, they took the stones out from under 'em an' left 'em down flat on the earth. An' the ruin o' this building, whatever it was, they rooted it out of it an' they put it out on the side o' the road to break for the road. But, the pile o' stones they put out, I s'pose there'd be about seventy or eighty yards o' stones in it. Now, when they were in the pile outside in the road not alone I, but several more besides me, heard something strange from that pile o' stones.

'Now, after dark when you'd be approachin' this heap, an' come within about ten or twelve yards of it, you'd hear the ring of a trowel, a mason's trowel, off the stones. An' sometimes you'd hear a dull thud, the same as if the trowel was full o' mortar. More times what you'd hear was like a bell, the ring o' the steel trowel. An' when you'd come up to the heap o' stones an' wait there — which I did, to know would I see anything or would the trowel start again — if you were there for forty years you couldn't hear it, or see anything. But yet when you went away ten or twelve yards from it the trowel started again. So I saw nothing, only heard the trowel. I can give no explanation where did the trowel come from except maybe that it had something to do with the stones bein' rooted out, that the masons that built the church came back when the stones were rooted, came back to warn the people that they did wrong by throwin' it out.

'How do I know 'twas a trowel I heard? Well, there was a firm in Sheffield, Braids Company, Sheffield; they used to make edged tools as well. An' the steel they used to put in 'em, I think that better couldn't be got. The mason's trowels they used to make, if you hit 'em against a stone they were like the ring of a bell. 'Twas those I heard. An' another firm that was makin' 'em in Sheffield was Spear and Jackson. They were good too. But the Braids, they were the best. A Braids trowel, if you got it, you could wear it to the handle, an' to bend it 'twould break. Tempered steel.

'But the pile o' stones. In about two months after, the breaker came on an' broke 'em up an' nothing was ever heard there after.'

'Below in Sixmilebridge these three, a brother an' his two sisters, they were living in a thatched house. Now, there was a right-angled turn in the road an' the road was sort o' straight down to this turn. But just where the road turned there was a gate an' inside the gate 'twas all in grass.

'But, at the time o' Brian Boru certain roads were made, an' I heard years ago that he made a road from Limerick to Galway, an' parts o' that road can be seen yet running through people's land. O' course there's grass growin' on the road now but you could see the two banks or walls in bits of it here an' there.

'These people I'm tellin' you about, they were livin' in an old thatched house by the side o' this old road. So, he had a brother in Australia who died an' left a lot o' money to him. When he got the money he decided to build a new house, an' where did he build the house but across the old road that was goin' out by the end of the house he was livin' in. I knew the two men that built it; they were from Cratloe. I saw 'em buildin' the house, an' they did all the carpentry work of it themselves, roofed it an' all. But when it came to the plastering o' the house, both inside an' outside, what plaster they'd put up today 'twas down on the ground tomorrow in a heap, an' they couldn't know what was wrong. In the finish up I think there were masses said in the house an' they were able to plaster it then.'

'But in all events, there was a man living below at Ráth Lúb cross, he's dead now for years, the Lord have mercy on his soul, whose name was Pat Pewter. Pat used to help this man, worked around the farm, an' that time there used to be fairs in Sixmilebridge. My man would maybe have one or two little cattle for the fair, an' the night before he'd ask Pat to go to the fair with him. An' the fairs at the time used to be at four o'clock in the morning, an' maybe sometimes earlier.

'But the night before the fair, anyway, Pat'd go down to him, in the evening around seven or eight o' clock, an' they wouldn't go to bed at all, only stay up by the fire all night. But, my man sez to him one night that they were sittin' at the fire

"'Well, Pat when you hear a knock at the back door go up from the fire, up in the middle o' the floor, or up near the door comin' in out o' the hall, or if you don't," sez he, "you'll be put up from it."

"'Faith then," sez Pat, "I won't go. I'll stay where I am an' I'll best whoever is in it."

"'All right," sez my man. "You can stay there, but I'm going up."

'Between twelve an' half past the knock came to the door an' my man took his chair an' went up in the middle o' the kitchen floor an' sat there.

"'Come up," sez he to Pat.

"'Faith then I won't go up." sez Pat to him, "I'll stay where I am."

'In three or four minutes Pat, chair, an' all, they were lifted from by the side o' the fire an' left down above near the man o' the house. So he said to Pat,

"'Didn't I tell you," sez he, "that you'd be put up from it? Because one night I was put up from it myself, chair an' all. An' I saw nothing," sez he.

"'Faith then," sez Pat, "I'll go to the fairs no more with you, now, because this house is haunted, it is, an' I won't come here any more," sez Pat.

'He didn't. So that was the story.'

'There's another haunted house a small piece from Kilkishen. 'Tis in a lonesome enough spot, too, at the end of a long boreen an' inside in a field. There was a single iron gate goin' into the yard of this house, an' who lived in the house in former years was a man whose name I won't mention. I'll just call him Jer. Well, this Jer, he was fond o' the beer. What porter he drank, 'twasn't barrels of it at all only lakes of it. He'd go to mass to Kilkishen, so I was told, an' after mass he'd fall in drinkin' there an' 'twould be some time that night when he'd leave it, maybe ten or eleven o' clock at night. When he'd be goin' home the road wasn't half wide enough for him an' he'd be keeping the two sides o' the road. An' if the road was forty miles wide 'twouldn't be wide enough for Jer after comin' out of the pub in Kilkishen.

'Anyway, when I saw this house, the last time I saw it, there wasn't a bit o' paint rubbed to the door. An' the front door if it was goin' out in a field, an' the back door was goin' into what appeared to be a yard, but the yard was growin' green grass. Outside the back door there was a stone flag an' the flag was as smooth as a sheet o' glass. The twenty-fourth o' June, 'tis the way that you'd want to be careful walkin' on that flag for fear you'd slip.

'But it happened, anyway, on the eleventh o' November. Poor Jer went to Kilkishen mass an' after mass he went into the pub. He drank his 'nuff there. Now, the same evenin' started freezin'. It started freezin' right hard. Anyway, poor Jer, when he'd be goin' to mass he used to hide the key of the door under a pot. When he'd go back he'd know where the key an' the pot was even if he was as drunk as that he wouldn't be able to stand.

'So this night in November he wobbled away home, an' I suppose it might take him two hours to go that short distance because he'd make the road about forty times longer than it would be. But he got the key anyway, an' 'twas freezin' heavens hard. I needn't tell you the way the smooth flag was outside the back door with the frost. He got the key under the pot, he went up on the flag to open the door, when the two legs were taken from under him above on the flag an' he came down on the flat of his back an' never again got up. His neighbour was goin' in countin' his cattle next day about ten o' clock an' he got him outside the back door, dead. He sent word to Tulla, to some relation of Jer's, that he got Jer dead outside the back door, an' probably he fell on the frosty flag an' broke his head.

'The man from Tulla came down, anyway, an' himself an' the man who found him brought in poor Jer an' brought him upstairs an' put him to bed — dead, o' course. They went to Kilkishen for the priest an' he came out an' prayed over him. They held a wake there that night. Next evenin' he was brought to Kilkishen church an' buried in Clonlea graveyard next day.

'A few years after that there was a man goin' around — I knew him — Tom Moloney was his name. He had no fixed abode, but the sort of a man he was that he might come to you, maybe in the winter time, or the harvest time, lookin' for a job. An' well an' good if you could give him the job; he'd take it. You might keep him for the winter, an' maybe the spring, but he was gone off some other place if you didn't want him.

'Now, there was a man livin' in the townland of Tyredagh, a farmer. An' 'twould be in the month o' November an' who came to him lookin' for a job only this Tom Moloney. Well, he came in the evenin', an' when he went in to the farmer's house they were eatin' the supper. The farmer asked him to have some supper, so he did. You see, Tom was with him before so they knew him well.

'"Tom," sez the farmer, "I've no place to put you up tonight, but," sez he, "you know where you'll go? There's a vacant house inside across the land an' if you go up," sez he, "to Tulla, I know the man that has the key of it. You can tell him that I sent you up. When you get it come down here again," sez he, "an' we'll go in."

'An' the same night was freezin', an' a moon up that you could pick pennies off the ground with it.

'When Tom Moloney had the supper ate he got up on his bicycle an' he hit for Tulla, up to the man that had the key, an' he told him that he got a job from the farmer in Tyredagh, an' that he was told by him that he had no place to put him up for the night but that there was a vacant house inside in the land an' he could stay in it only to get the key.

'"Oh, begod there is," sez my man, "and I have the key of it."

'"That's what I came for," sez Tom.

'"I'll give it to you," sez he.

'So he gave him the key of Jer's house. Tom, anyway, got up on the bike an' he hit back to Tyredagh again. When he went back he told the farmer that he got the key.

'"Bedad," sez the farmer, "I'll get a bit, now, for your breakfast before you come out in the morning. An' everything else is in the house," sez he. "There's bedclothes, ware, cups, saucers, mugs, jugs, plates, everything. You'll be short o' nothing. All you're short of," sez he, "is the bit to eat, an' I'll get that for you. And," sez he, "we'll bring two bags, an' we'll collect a bit o' turf goin' out the yard an' we'll put down a fire. Then we can go upstairs an' get the bedclothes. But they weren't slept in since the house was closed so I suppose they're soakin' in dampness."

'Anyway, he got a bit for Tom's breakfast an' they got two bags an' started out. They collected two bags o' turf goin' out the yard an' went into the house. They put down a fire o' turf in the kitchen an' when 'twas well lighted they went upstairs an' brought down the bed-clothes. An' Tom Moloney took particular notice that there was an old dresser in the kitchen with dishes, cups, mugs, jugs, knives, forks, plates. Everything was there; a table in the middle o' the floor, chairs.

'But, they dried the bedclothes, brought down mattress an' all an' dried the lot an' warmed 'em well. Then they brought 'em up again an' settled the bed — 'twas over the kitchen. The farmer stayed with him then until, I suppose, around eleven o' clock. They were talkin' at the fire. Then he said that he'd go. So, "You needn't be out, Tom," sez he, "too early tomorrow. Dhera, I s'pose around ten or eleven o' clock will do you. An' I'll have your dinner for you when you come out. An' I'll have a bed for you," sez he, "tomorrow night, outside. You can bring out the key o' this place when you're comin' an' one of us can take it up to Tulla again."

'Anyway, he went away. Tom Moloney went to bed an' he wasn't very long in bed when he heard noise below in the kitchen. 'Twas the very self an' same as if you started rolling around the kitchen an empty tar barrel. It went up the stairs an' into the room where Tom was in bed, in under the bed, an' turned Tom an' the bed upside down on the floor. Tom came out from under the bed. His clothes were on a chair, an' as it was a moonlit night he got his clothes, out the room door, down the stairs with his clothes an' boots in his hand, an' out the back door an' the night freezin'. He was the lucky man he didn't brain himself on the same flag that Jer got killed on.

'He put on his clothes an' boots an' socks outside in the green yard at the back o' the house, an' out he went across the land, out to the farmer's. He went around the house an' he called on 'em to let him in. An' the farmer stuck his head out the top window.

'"Who's there?" sez he.

'"Tom Moloney. In the name o' God will you let me in!"

'"In the honour o' God, what are you doin' this hour o' the morning?"

'"O, let me in," sez he, "I wouldn't stay in that house another hour. If you gave me forty pounds," sez he, "I wouldn't stay in it another hour."

'"Hold on," sez he, "till I go down, till I let you in."

'Down the stairs with him an' he let him in. He sat by the fire until the followin' morning, until the whole family got up. An' he told 'em all that if he got forty pounds he wouldn't stay in that house another hour, that 'twas haunted.

'Tom Moloney told that story himself. I was listenin' to him. An' I was tellin' a friend o' mine in Sean Daingean, some time after, that if he'd come with me I'd stay in the house for one night. An' you know what he said?

'"In the name o' God," sez he, "Jimmy, keep away as far as ever you can from it, because," sez he, "you could be got dead in it in the morning."

'So I didn't go near it.'

'Faith, Quin has a place like that too. The old barrack in Quin, 'twas originally owned by Michael O'Dea but when he left it 'twas closed for a while an' then the guards got it. But, there was a guard from Buttevant there, an' himself an' I were the best o' friends, so I used to ramble up in the winter nights to 'em from Bally-roughan.

'This winter night, anyway, I was inside in the barrack, an' I s'pose about nine o' clock, right over the day-room where I was talkin' with two o' the guards, the walking started overhead.

'"Who in the name o' goodness," sez I, "is above stairs?"

'"Take no notice o' that," sez one of 'em to me. "It isn't the first time that was heard there."

'Well, 'twould be like a heavy person walking on the

first floor, a boarded floor. The house was an old one.

'The guard said to me, anyway, "I'll tell you one now," sez he, "and 'tis only last week it happened. I was here," sez he, "one night on my own, reading a book. An' 'twas an incandescent oil lamp now, one o' them aladdin lamps, that I had. But, I had the lamp," sez he, "left on the table an' the table in front o' the fire, an' I was sitting exactly there at the right-hand side o' the fireplace as you'd face it. I was reading a book. As you know," sez he, "I like an odd pull o' the pipe. Well, I put my hand in my pocket," sez he, "for the tobacco an' the pipe as I got anxious for a smoke. I left the book open an' turned it upside down on the table so as it wouldn't close or the pages to go from where I was readin'. I filled the pipe, anyway, an' I got a bit o' the edge of a newspaper to light it. An' I stood off the chair an' lighted the paper," sez he, "from the fire. When I sat back 'tis a wonder," sez he, "that I didn't break my back because 'twas down on the floor I sat. The chair was gone. No explanation! Now, the next day," sez he, "that chair was got upstairs, in the room overhead, an' 'twas one o' the other lads here that got it. You know him well enough yourself. Ask him an' he'll tell you about it."

'I did, an' he told me he found it there, all right.'

'There's something about Granahan castle too. I heard several people say that between Fenloe an' Ballycar there's a small townland called Granahan. Did you ever hear tell of it? Well now, there's a big lake opposite Fenloe blessed well an' there's a tail of that lake goin' down very near the railway below Ballycar. But at the edge o' the lake — I didn't see it myself, now — at the edge o' the lake there was a castle called Granahan castle. Well, only the foundations of it were there. Anyway, I heard that every seven years a person would blow a bugle at Granahan castle an' 'tis only one or two persons that would hear it. But anybody that'd hear it, they were gone to the next world before that bugle would sound the following seven years. An' I heard that the last person that heard it was Ned Hewitt in Granahan, an' in three years after he died.'

'No, I didn't hear anything strange about Mountcashel castle, but what I did hear was that people used to hear noises below near it. Just below Tierney's gate, at the right, there's a quarry an' I heard that often at twelve o'clock in the night people used to be heard workin' in that quarry with shovels an' bars, the same as they would in the middle o' the day. An' no one ever saw anything there, only heard the bars an' the shovels workin'. Shouldn't something unusual happen there at some time to account for them goings-on?'

6. Strange Encounters

'Long ago people used to see things at night that'd never be seen now. An' I saw things myself that I wouldn't want to see anymore. An' why aren't they seen now? I'll tell you why, an' there's two good reasons for that. You might think that the electricity is one of 'em, but 'tisn't. One reason is that people are goin' everywhere in cars these days an' they have no time to see anything. But the real reason, I think, is the paths; no one is usin'.the paths an' short-cuts through the land now compared to the gangs o' people that were usin' 'em years ago. There wasn't hardly a field where people usedn't travel, day an' night. An' now, there's no one travellin' 'em at all.

'I'll tell you, now, what happened me several times when I was out on them paths at night, an' a few other things I heard about other people too.

'Christy Cullinan's in Kilcornan, they used to be gamblin' there an' I used to go over. Although I usedn't to gamble myself — I used to play, you know, at home all right but never played outside — I used to go over watchin' 'em. So, 'twould be, I suppose, sometime before Christmas, an' the moon was up, an' the gamble broke up between eleven an' half eleven. Myself an' one o' the gamblers, we started for home, an' walkin' we were. After comin' out o' Christy Cullinan's 'twas up a steep hill, now, that was in Kilcornan road, an' down the other side. Well now, from Ballyroughan lake there was a trench goin' over between Grace's in Kincornan an' McMahon's in Newmarket. This trench was comin' over to the road an' where it was joinin' the road 'twas an acute angle. An' the drain was goin' along by the side o' the road for, I s'pose, about a hundred yards. Now, where it was comin' out to the road 'twas lower than the road an' there were two flat stones, one at each side of it, an' you could step across the two flat stones an' up into McMahon's crag.

'But as it was a fine moonlit night, an' the same night was freezin', I said to my man, "Begod, I'll go up across McMahon's place. 'Tis a lot shorter way," sez I, "than goin' around by the cross, goin' around by Ráth Lúb. Good night, then," sez I to him.

'"Good night, Jimmy," sez he, "I'll go 'way this way."'

'He walked away. I went down to the flat stone, stepped across, up the other side into McMahon's crag. Now, there was a clump o' bushes in the crag about five or six hundred yards up, an' I was about half way between the drain an' the clump o' bushes when I saw what appeared to me to be . . . did you ever see an old, common horse-creel for drawin' turf? Well now, you can imagine that you took the horse creel off the car, put it together on the ground an' threw a black cloak or a black rug over it . . . It appeared to me to be about that way, an' 'twas movin' towards me from the bushes at a very slow pace. When I saw it, I don't know what kind of a spin I gave but back I went, back to the drain or trench, down on the two flat stones an' up the other side. An' I thought I'd break my legs runnin' around by the cross. I went around the road up home an' that finished me crossin' that way at night.

'I met my gamblin' man the followin' evenin' an' I was tellin' him about what happened.

'"D'you ever hear, Jimmy," sez he, "that the longest way round is the shortest way home?"

'Did anything ever happen there? Well, in former years there was a man killed there comin' down the hill; O'Brien was his name. Killed accidentally. Now, this O'Brien man had a bit of a garden beyond in Kilcornan an' he generally used to sow mangolds an' potatoes in the garden — but there'd be no more than, I s'pose, half an acre in it. One day, anyway, he was drawin' manure over for the potatoes an' he was comin' back with the empty car, standin' above in the car. An' a pony he had. But it seems that when he was goin' up Kilcornan hill one side o' the breeching opened, an' when he got up to the top o' the hill the pony got into a trot. The car was runnin' out on the pony an' he started goin' faster, an' O'Brien pullin' on the reins, holdin' back the pony. Goin' down near the bottom o' the hill one side o' the reins opened an' what did he do but pulled on the other side an' the horse turned in on the ditch. There was a high ditch at the time on the side o' the road an' one o' the wheels o' the car went up on it an' turned the car upside down on top o' the poor man an' killed him.

'So that might have something to do with what I saw that night.'

'Another night I was listening to a band that was playin' in a house in Ballycar, an' when they broke up an' went away a couple o' the lads an' I, we came out an' walked down as far as Ballycar cross an' went over the railway bridge. We stood at the cross, anyway, for about ten minutes talkin', an' then one of 'em said to me, "Bedad, Jimmy," sez he, "you have a nice bit of a road to go. An' we'll be goin' ourselves too."

'They went anyway an' I got up on the bike an' cycled away. An' comin' over just beyond Fenloe blessed well there's a kind of a rise in the road. Now, the sort of a place it was, there'd be maybe three or four yards of a sharp incline up in the road an' 'twas level then on top for about seven or eight yards; then there was a fall down again for three or four yards, a sharp kind of a fall. But what I suggest it was: at the left-hand side as I was comin' to Ballyroughan there was a pump-house inside in the field, that Major Hickman had when he owned Fenloe, an' I suggest that it was the water pipes, d'you see, going out from the pump-house to the lake, an' the workmen that built it made this kind of a thing over 'em; they were under the road an' they had this sort of a bridge made over 'em, that rose the road.

'But anyway, when I was comin' on the bike, goin' down the fall at the other side, didn't the dynamo on the bike quench, went out of a shot!

'"In the name o' goodness," sez I in my own mind, "the bulb is gone."

'The night was dark. I left my leg on the road when the bulb went — as I thought — 'cos I could see nothing. An' just beyond the blessed well, now, between the blessed well an' a gate goin' into the graveyard, there's a wall about four feet high, with flat stones on top of it. An' above on the wall what do you think I saw?

'Now, the best way I could describe 'em to you, Eddie . . . they'd be about the size of two dinner plates, circular. They were the very same, now, as two plates of iron that you'd be after takin' out of a coal fire, pure red. An' they were above on top o' the wall, about a foot apart.

'When I saw 'em I started the prayer that the priest used to say after mass long ago:

Blessed Michael the archangel, defend us in the hour o' battle, be our safeguard against the wickedness an' snares o' the devil . . .

When I said that prayer I saw the two of 'em fallin' in over the wall into the field, an' when I was passin' where they were 'twas the very same as if there was a big fire at either side o' the road. There was a wave o' heat across the road. I leant on the pedals o' the bike, an' 'tis a wonder that between that an' home that the oul' bike didn't fall asunder. I got a fright that night, all right.'

'Now, there was the figure of a black man seen in Dromulla, an' he was supposed to be one of the Bridgemans of Ráth Lúb. According to some o' the local people they were still knockin' around there. According to my aunt those Bridgemans canvassed for Daniel O'Connell in the Clare election of 1829, but they got broken in the canvassing.

'Well, I can't say whether 'tis from the fort that's in Ráth Lúb or not that this black man appears. But 'twould be between, I'd say, one o'clock and half-one at Ballyroughan, where the fort is, that he comes through thick white-thorn bushes an' crosses the road into Ballyroughan hill. An' where he goes in there's the formation of a ruin of an old house there. 'Tis a sort of a hollow that's in the bottom o' the hill an' in the winter time 'tis full o' water. The deepest 'twould be is about three feet, but in the summer time 'tis quite dry.

'One winter . . . 'twould be before Christmas, 1937, they used to be gamblin' at Martin Grady's. An' I left the gamble when 'twas broken up around one o'clock. I had a bicycle so I got up on the bike an' cycled away home. Goin' up Callaghan's hill — 'tis a very steep hill — I had to get off the bicycle an' walk up. But on top o' the hill, anyway, I got on the bike, an' I was cyclin' away, never suspecting anything.

'I was gone about two hundred yards when, I s'pose, 'twouldn't be four feet away from the front wheel this tall man dressed in black, wearin' a hat, crossed the road. As far as I could judge, now, in the night the hat an' the clothes were jet black. But, he crossed into this hole o' water an' he made no more a sound in the water no more than a mouse. He took no notice o' me. But when I saw him I left my leg on the road. I pulled the brake an' left my leg on the road. An' he'd be no more than about four feet away from the front wheel o' the bike. I thought at the time, o' course, that he was a real man.

'About three or four nights after that there was a

motor pulled up at the gate, just above it, when I was goin' home the same way. An' curiosity made me go over to see who was in the car. Who was it only the priest from Sixmilebridge. When I went over he sez to me, "In the name o' goodness, Jimmy, where are you comin' from this hour o' the night?"

"'Comin' up from a bit of a gamble, Father," sez I. "What time is it?"

'He looked at the watch.

"'Twenty past twelve," sez he. "An' d'you know, Jimmy," sez he, "you shouldn't be out so late."

"'Dhera, Father," sez I, "they were talkin' below, bedad."

"'Tell me," sez he, "did you hear anything, or ever see anything like a black man that's supposed to be seen around here?"

"'Bedad, Father, 'tis only about . . . what night is this?" sez I. "I think 'twas Tuesday night last that I saw him."

"'An' where were you comin' from?" sez he to me.

"'Down from a gamble," sez I, "that was at Martin Grady's. I was watchin' 'em up there."

"'Well, what time would that be?" sez he.

"'I'll tell you, Father," sez I. "When I went in home I looked at the clock an' 'twas twenty past one."

"'But Jimmy," sez he, "don't be comin' at that particular time past that spot any more. An' if I see this black man I'll put him," sez he, "where he won't come out of any more."

"'Could you tell me, Father," sez I, "who is he or what is he?"

"'Jimmy," sez he, "all I can tell you about him is that he's from the other world . . . that's all I can tell you. Who he is or what he is I don't know. But he's from the other world."

'But, I never heard of him bein' seen there after that,

so maybe the priest did do something.'

'My grandfather, he used to go to the gamble below at Stephen Mac's where they used to gamble for geese an' turkeys. But, when he'd be goin' home, maybe at one o' clock when 'twould break up, he had to pass up this fort that the road was made through a bit of, d'you see. An' right before him he often saw a black dog. He used to come out through the bushes, out of the fort, an' go up the road before him for, I s'pose, two hundred yards. An' there was water out of a spring that was in the hill at the left-hand side o' the road. 'Twas crossin' the road, runnin' in a little stream, d'you see, over the road. The roads weren't tarred at all that time. But this black dog would go just as far as that stream, an' disappear there.

'But several nights he saw that black dog. An' whatever kind of a thing it was it appears it couldn't cross the spring water. So 'twas no ordinary dog, whatever else it might be.'

'Now, d'you remember me tellin' you about this guard in Quin that I was great friends with? Well, I used to repair bicycles for him, an' for all the guards in Quin, an' I was well known by all of 'em.

'But one night, anyway, I went up to this guard's house, an' he was gettin' milk from a farmer in Daingean Breac at the time, an' he sez to me about eight o' clock, "Begod, Jimmy, you know what you'll do? Get the tin can there an' go over," sez he, "for the milk for me for tomorrow."

'"Bedad I will," sez I.

'I had the bicycle left outside the front door an' I got the tin can an' hit off for Daingean Breac. I was just below the church cross when . . . I would say, now, 'twas only inside the road wall that the crying started. An' it started something like this, now: "aaaaa-

AAAuuu! aaaaaAAAuuu! aaaaaAAAuuu!"

'Well, as sure as you're there, Eddie, I nearly broke the chain o' the oul' bike from there to where I was goin' for the milk. In the yard with me an' into the kitchen with the tin can in my hand. An' when I went in my man an' a man he had workin' for him were there. When they saw the state o' me one of 'em sez to me, "Begod, Jimmy, you appear to be frightened."

'"Oh, in the name o' God," sez I, "I'm after hearin' the most mournful cry beyond there in the road."

'"Goodness sake," sez he, "don't be foolish. Yourself an' your cryin'!"

'Next thing, didn't a neighbour of theirs come in.

'"Come out," sez he, "until ye hear the banshee."

'The whole lot of us went out in the yard, an' down below Moylan's, in Feequin, we heard the cry goin' out towards Cullane, an' then it faded away.

'The next evenin' I came up to that house again around four o' clock to know did they find out what it was, an' when I came up the man o' the house sez to me, "Are you goin' to the funeral?"

'"Who's dead?" sez I.

'"A great friend o' yours," sez he, "over in Crevagh is dead, an' he's goin' to the church this evenin'. I'm goin' to the funeral an' you'll be with me."

'The two of us got bicycles an' hit for the funeral, an' we met it comin', half way between Crevagh an' Quin. So that's one o' my experiences o' the banshee.'

'I was below at a house in Sean Daingean one evenin', an' I was standin' at the door, an' right inside across the road from where I was — I s'pose 'twould be no more than twenty yards — there was a sod wall between the field an' the road. I would say that 'twas just inside the wall the cry started, "aaaaaAAAAAAaa! aaaaaA-AAAaa!"

94

'I turned back into the house.

'"In heaven's name," sez I, "what's that?"

'"Oh," sez the man inside, "we heard it as well. That's the banshee. There must be someone dead around the place."

'Next evenin' the account came that an old man was dead in the County Home in Ennis. An' that same old man lived in that cottage before the man I was talkin' to got it. So that's another experience o' the banshee.

'What I heard was that the banshee followed families whose surnames began with the third an' seventh letters of the alphabet, that's "C" and "G". But I also heard that she followed families whose names were "O" or "Mac".

'Someone told me, too, about the banshee that in olden times rich families in Ireland, they used to pay a woman to cry when a member o' the family would be dead, an' these women were known as keeners or criers. Well, these criers are heard when a member o' that family dies. I heard that.'

'Something else like that happened some years ago when I used to go in to various houses on a *cuaird* every night. This night I went down to Callagahan's, down to Ráth Lúb cross an' who came in after me only the next door neighbour. An' there were more neighbours inside. They were sittin' at the fire an' talkin', an' I needn't tell you that in those times, in the houses, nearly what'd be happened in three or four counties would be discussed.

'But, about eleven o' clock the man o' the house said that he was goin' to bed, that he had to get up in the mornin' to go up to Studdert's in Cullane, workin'. So we all came out, an' o' course he conveyed us as far as the gate. An' outside the door there was a little triangular bit of a green. We stood in the green, talkin', an' the next thing we heard was all this screeching. Now, the best way I could describe it, 'twas like an oul' common car that didn't see a drop of oil or a bit o' grease for about forty years, an' 'twas comin' through Littleton's place in Sean Daingean. The man o' the house said to the rest of us, "Come in," sez he, "an' let that pass, whatever it it. An' I don't know," sez he, "what road 'twill take. But come back! Come in! That's the *cóiste bodhar* if 'tis in Ireland."

'We all went in, anyway, into the house an' shut the door. An' the next thing was that we didn't hear it at all. So when it stopped we went out again, out in the green. An' goin' up Ballyroughan Hill it started again. That was my place. It faded out, anyway, faded away an' we heard no more of it or saw no more an' I went away up home. That's that.

'An ordinary sidecar? How would it be? Wouldn't we have it seen.

'Now there were roads made in Ireland at the time o' Brian Boru; I told you that already, didn't I? An' people have shown me a part of a road that was made at that time from Limerick to Galway. Bits of it are there yet, all right. An' 'tis said that the *cóiste bodhar* travels those roads. Not always, now, but occasionally.

'Those few things I'm after tellin' you, they happened to myself, but wait, now, an' you'll hear what happened to other people, some of whom I knew an' others I heard about.

'These two men were livin' in Quin — their grandchildren are there yet — their names were Pat an' Tom. They had land over on the Ard Solas road an' they used always keep a pair o' working horses. But, one o' the horses was gettin' old an' Pat decided that he'd buy one, an' the best place that he thought he'd get a working horse was at the fair o' Spancil Hill. Now, the horsefair in Spancil Hill would be on the twenty-third o' June, an' the cattle fair on the twenty-fourth. But anyway, the night o' the twenty-second Pat an' Tom, they left Quin on a horse an' sidecar.

'Why didn't they go in the morning? The fairs at Spancil Hill, an' all the fairs at that time, they used to be held generally at day-break in the morning. To get the choice you'd have to be there early.

'But they left Quin about eleven o'clock. They had about eight miles to go to Spancil Hill an' 'twould be, I s'pose, about three miles from Spancil Hill to Clooney graveyard. They went up by Hazelwood, on by Claí a' tSeascadh an' up to Clooney. Now, Tom he was sitting at the left-hand side o' the sidecar an' Pat was sitting at the right-hand side driving the horse. Tom, anyway, was at the graveyard side going over an' when they were passing Clooney graveyard gate he saw a man there, standing reading a book, at that time o' night.

'So they had passed the graveyard an' Tom said to Pat, "There was a man standing," sez he, "at the gate, reading a book. I'll go back," sez he, "an' see what he wants."

'"If you take my advice," sez Pat to him, "you wouldn't go back."

'"I will," sez Tom.

'Pat pulled up the horse an' Tom got down an' went back. He sez to the man, "What are you doin' there," sez he, "at this hour o' the night readin' that book?"

'"Work your day," sez the man, "an' sleep your night, an' let the evil take its flight."

'He said no more. Tom walked away on to where Pat was an' got on the side-car. They went to the fair o'Spancil Hill, Pat bought a horse an' brought him back to Quin. An' when they arrived in Quin Tom went home an' went into bed, an' couldn't get out of it for a month after because his two knees were as weak as he couldn't straighten 'em.

'The fellow they met was from the other world, surely.'

'I knew another man, too, that wasn't in the better of meeting the good people. He was livin' below in Sean Daingean an' workin' at Kilcornan. Now, from the top of Kilcornan Hill over to his cottage there was one field belonging to the Littleton's in Sean Daingean, an' every evenin' when he'd break off work he'd go into a neighbouring house an' they used to be playin' cards there. He'd join in the gamble when he'd go in an' it might be maybe twelve o'clock when they'd break up. Many is the night that he went in the stile above on top o' Kilcornan Hill, down across Littleton's field an' out below another stile in front of his own cottage an' in home.

'But 'twas a moonlit night this night; 'twould be in the month o' January. He told me this himself. He came out o' where he was workin' after his supper, into the gamblin' house, took part in the gamble, an' they played away there until about a quarter to twelve, when it broke up. He came over the road an' when he came up to the top o' the hill he went in the stile an' the next thing was, he saw all these little men, small little men, an' they playin' football inside in the field. He didn't know who they were or what they were. He walked down through 'em. There were hundreds of 'em in it an' they playin' football in the moonlight. But they never spoke, nor he never spoke. He went in home an' went into bed an' the followin' mornin' he wasn't able to get up. He was as weak, he told me, as a drink o' water. The wife gave him the breakfast in the bed, an' the dinner, an' he couldn't stand or walk for a week after. The man that he was workin' for came over for him, to know why wasn't he goin' to work. He told him his story an' he was told stay in bed. He got up in about a week after an' he was perfect. He didn't come across that field any more at night.'

'The exact same thing happened to the son of a very good friend o' mine, but 'twasn't the good people that he met, but somethin' else. He told me he was workin' for a big farmer in Ballykilty an' every evenin' he'd have his supper there. An' at that time they used to be playin' cards at a house in Kildrum — 'twould be in the winter time, o' course. After his supper, now, he'd come out the front avenue o' the place where he was workin' an' down to Glynn's bridge in Ballykilty. Goin' in at the bridge there was a stile in the wall, an' the stile, o' course, 'twas two long stones put down on their edge. I s'pose they'd be about a foot wide in the bottom an' about three feet wide in the top. You know those. An animal couldn't get through 'em.

'As well as that one, then, there was another one in a sod wall down to a drain that was goin' under the road. But there was another wall at the other side o' that field with another stile, an' outside that, then, was a crag. 'Twas a crag, now, that was at the right o' the road as you'd be goin' out to Kildrum or Knappogue. Out again on the road, nearly opposite Clune's gate there was another stile, an' I s'pose he had no more than about two or three hundred yards to go from that stile down to the house where they used to be playin' the cards.

'Anyway, 'twould be around maybe twelve o'clock in the night when they'd break up the gamble. So, one night this man came up the road, up as far as the stile that was opposite Clune's gate, an' went in the stile an' across the crag, along by the bank o' this little stream. The second stile was going into the potato garden where the old woman worked the piseógs — d'you remember me tellin' you about that? Well, there was a flat stone on top o' the wall at the left-hand side, now, as you'd be approaching the stile from the Kildrum road. There was a big flat stone on top o' the wall, an' sittin' on this big flat stone there was a white cat, an' the cat ran along the top o' the wall. An' where you'd never see or hear of a cat goin' was into a trench o' water, but didn't he hear the splash in the water, an' see no more or hear no more. He went away home, went to bed.

'The followin' few nights the same thing happened. The cat used to be in it when he'd be goin' home some time between twelve an' half-twelve. Now, at the time they used to break stones with a hammer for the roads, an' there was a heap o' stones broken just above the stile that was opposite Clune's gate. Anyway, when he went to the stile he just thought to himself, "If the cat is there tonight," sez he, "the cat won't be there tomorrow night because I'll introduce some o' these stones to him."

'He went up to the heap o' stones an' filled his two coat pockets with the stones out o' the heap. An' I suppose some o' the stones, there'd be a pound weight in 'em.

'But, he went in the stile anyway, an' down the crag, an' sure enough, when he was approachin' the second stile the cat was in it, an' he came within, I s'pose about ten or twelve yards o' the cat. He took out a rock out of his pocket, one in each hand an' he let fly at the cat.

'"An' faith," sez he to me when he was tellin' me the story, "I should be fairly near him because with one spring," sez he, "he was straight into the trench o' water, an' 'twas the same as if I threw the flat rock that was on top o' the wall into the stream, into the water, the splash that he made. I went down home, went into bed, an' the followin' night again I went up across the four stiles, up to the gamblin' house. An' 'twas the same time," sez he, "that the gamble broke up; I s'pose around twelve. I went up the road an' in the stile at Clune's gate an' down the crag, down along by the bank o' the little trench. An' faith," sez he, "when I was comin' to the second stile there was no cat there. I went out the second stile, an' I had gone," sez he, "about twenty yards out the field when I heard a low whisper say 'Go back'."

"'I went about twenty yards farther when I heard the voice again say 'Go back!' I went out the third stile, an' after goin' out the third stile, out in Glynn's field, I was held up altogether an' I could hear distinctly, 'GO BACK!' I turned round where I was an' went back the three stiles again, an' up around by the school, up around the road, up to Hassett's cross an' down the Ballykilty road. But when I was goin' down Halloran's hill," he said, "down near the bottom o' the hill there did a girl pass me on the road, dressed in white. I never laid eyes on her before in my life. An' when I passed her," sez he, "'twas the very self an' same as if I passed a big fire on the road. I started to sweat, an' every step I was takin' until I went down home," sez he, "'twas worse I was gettin'. The shirt was stuck to my back with sweat. When I went in home I looked into the looking-glass. I couldn't imagine," sez he, "that I was really sweatin'. When I looked into the looking-glass 'twas the very self an' same as if a one threw a bucket o' water over me. I took off my shirt," sez he, "an' squeezed it, put on a dry shirt on me, an' went into bed, an' next day I wasn't able to get out of it. My father," sez he, "brought me in my breakfast an' when I had the breakfast eaten I threw it up again."

"'There was a priest in Quin," sez he, "Fr Smith, an' my father went for him. An' he came, an' whatever he did, in two or three days I was as well as ever I was. An' that's what I got, now, for peltin' the cat that was on the second stile. 'Twasn't a cat at all," sez he. "I don't know what it was but 'twasn't a cat, anyway, only something in the appearance of a cat."

'That's the story he told me. An' I'd say 'twas the

same cat the lads met in Ballykilty fort the night they were searchin' for the gold.'

'A man below in Kilkishen was tellin' me that the Dunboynes in Knappogue, they were freemasons, an' that they used to hold meetings, but they couldn't hold the meetings without thirteen members bein' there. Now, the Bloods in Ballykilty, an' the Studderts in Cullane, of course they were Protestants, an' the Studderts in Hazelwood, Mahon in Corbally an' Power in Brooke Lodge, all them were Protestants. An' I heard that they used to be at the freemasons' meetings too.

'But they held a meeting, anyway, in Knappogue, an' there was a man from Kilkishen, John Dobbyn was his name. He was before the Studderts came to Kilkishen, an' he was another Protestant. But he was to be at the meeting but he had gone on a journey the day that they were to hold the meeting, the freemason meeting, in Knappogue. Twelve of 'em turned up but Dobbyn, you see, wasn't back in time. Anyway, when he wasn't turnin' up at the appointed time they said that they'd hold the meeting without him. So the twelve went up to the freemason room that was at the top o' the stone stairs, an' whatever devilment they were goin' on there I was told that the whole castle started shiverin' an' shakin'. When 'twas shiverin' an' shakin' didn't Dobbyn arrive an' came in the door below, an' as soon as he went in below the thing stopped. Up the stairs he went an' into the room where they were. An' when he went in he abused 'em for not waitin' until he came. He told 'em that if he hadn't come the whole castle'd have fallen down on top of 'em.

'Did you ever see the stone stairs in Knappogue castle? In every step of that stairs there's a print of a bare foot, going up. The toes are turned in. The five toes, they're there the same as if they were chiselled in it, an' how they came there I don't know. 'Tis the same, now, I could say, as if you put your foot into water an' left it down on a concrete floor, that shape. On every step o' the stairs.'

'There was only one man I heard of that did any good out o' meeting strange fellows at night, an' that was Tom Burke the bone-setter. O' course there's a lot o' stories about how he got the gift, but one I remember hearing is that he went out one night, he was on some journey, an' when he was goin' home 'twould be in the middle o' the night. He met a funeral, anyway, an' three men carryin' a coffin. One o' the men that was carryin' the coffin on his shoulders, he asked him to know would he give 'em a help. They had one man at one end of it an' the two more at the other side. So he went in with the single man, of course, two an' two, to carry the coffin, an' they brought the coffin to a graveyard. They brought it into the graveyard, left it down an' one o' the men that was carryin' it, he said to him, "Thank you very much," sez he, "Mr Burke," callin' him by his name. An' he said to him, "Whatever request, now, that you'll ask 'twill be granted to you."

'"Well, I'll tell you now," sez Tom Burke, "what I'd like to be able to do. A lot o' people suffer with frac-tured bones an' dislocated bones, an' I'd like to be able," sez he, "to set 'em an' put 'em back."

'"That request," sez the man, "will be granted to you."

'So the three men disappeared an' ever after Tom Burke was able to put back dislocated bones an' set broken bones. So that's how I heard that he got it.

'There was a son of his an' he was an expert at it too, an' I think there's a daughter of his that can do it.'

7. Strongholds of the Good People

'There must be hundreds o' forts in the whole county o'
Clare. Sure, won't you get one in nearly every townland, an' more in some of 'em. I don't know did the
fairies ever live in 'em or not, but someone lived in 'em.
An' I wouldn't like to see 'em being done away with
because I would say that they can tell us something
about the way the people long ago lived. An', o' course,
a lot o' people wouldn't touch 'em because they believe
'tis not a right thing. I heard a lot o' stories about people
that interfered with forts an' hadn't a day's luck after.
There's other things, too. You remember the lads
searchin' for the gold at Ballykilty fort?

'Here's one for you, now. Johnny Pewter lived at
Creag a' tSeascadh an' he was very fond o' shootin'. An'
there was a lone man livin' at Corbally cross at the time
whose name was Pat Lacy, an' Pat used to go with
Johnny when he'd be goin' shooting. But, one time they
went over by Caherlohan, an' maybe back by Toona an'
Clooney, an' from Clooney down by Corbally. Of
course, all this journey'd be across the country. Anyway, 'twas dusk in the evenin' — 'twas in the month o'
November — an' they were comin' down across the
country an' they came by Corbally fort. Now, Corbally
fort is a double-ring fort on top of a hill. There were two
rows o' bushes, anyway, white-thorn bushes, big whitethorn bushes, growin' on the two banks o' the fort.
When Johnny Pewter an' Pat Lacy were passing out the
fort Pat sez to Johnny, "Johnny," sez he, "d'you see the
big bird inside in the bush. An' that bird," sez he, "is
surely as big as a goose."

'Johnny looked in.

'"Where's the bird?" sez he. "I see no bird."

'"Gimme that gun," sez Pat, "until I shoot him."

'Johnny gave him the gun. He let bang in through the bush, an' the bird fluttered down through the bush. Pat handed back the gun again to Johnny, went down on his two knees an' went in under the bush to get the bird that he shot. An' when he went into the butt o' the bush there was nothing there only a heap o' suds. So, bedad, he turned out.

'"By God, Johnny," sez he, "there's nothing here only suds."

'"Come away from it," sez Johnny.

'The two of 'em went away. Pat Lacy went in home an' Johnny went home. About eleven the next day Johnny came again for Pat to go with him. Sure, when he arrived at Pat's house Pat was inside in bed. An' he sez to Johnny through the bedroom window, "Johnny," sez he, "I got up this mornin' to make a bit o' breakfast for myself an' I staggered around the room. I wasn't able to stand. I went back into bed again. An' begod," sez he, "I might as well give you the key. You'll come in an' you might make a drop o' tea for me. I'd drink it."

'He threw Johnny the key out the window an' Johnny opened the door, went into the room to him, an' they had a chat inside.

'"Have the drop o' tea now, Pat," sez he. "Then I'll go to Quin for the doctor an' see what he'll do for you."

'"Begod, do," sez Pat.

'Johnny went away, anyway an' went to Quin, an' in about an hour after the doctor arrived in a horse an' sidecar. He went in an' he had a chat with Pat.

'"Pat," sez he, "you're fairly bad. Get up an' I'll help you to put on your clothes an' I'll bring you," sez he, "to Garruragh hospital."

''Twas known that time as Garruragh workhouse, an' that workhouse was between Tulla an' Ballinahinch.

'So anyway, the doctor, he brought Pat Lacy to the

workhouse an' he was taken in there an' he was put into a ward an' into bed. The doctor went away. About twelve o'clock that night, or half-twelve, four men went into the ward carrying a coffin. They left the coffin down by the side o' Pat Lacy's bed an' one o' the men that was carryin' the coffin said to Pat, "Get up out o' that bed," sez he, "an' pick the shot out o' my brother that you shot yesterday at Corbally fort. Or if you don't pick 'em out of him," sez he, "you'll never get out of it alive."

'So Pat got up an' he started pickin' the grains o' shot out o' the man in the coffin, an' when he had the last grain picked out of him the man in the coffin got up an' came out o' the coffin. One o' the other lads put on the cover on it an' screwed it down an' the five of 'em disappeared through the hospital wall, coffin an' all. Next morning Pat was as well as ever he was. He was discharged from the hospital, an' went to America after. So that's one story about a fairy fort.'

'Wait now. There was another story, too, about that fort, Corbally fort. This Brian O'Brien was from Castleconnell in the County Limerick. Anyway, every November Eve himself an' John Gorman that lived in Corbally, they used to listen to the grandest music that was ever heard on the bagpipes comin' from Corbally fort or that direction. That'd be at about twelve o'clock November Eve. But one November Eve Brian O'Brien said to John Gorman as they were listening to it, "I'll go up," sez he, "an' see where 'tis coming from an' try an' find out who's playin' it."

'John Gorman, anyway, tried to persuade him not to go but he persisted an' went. Now, out a bit from the fort, in the side o' the hill, didn't he see a faint light protruding through the ground. He went up to it, up to this light as he thought, an' he saw an opening into a tunnel. He went in, an' as he was goin' in the light was gettin' brighter. Then he came to the entrance to a big room. He went to the entrance an' there was a big blazin' fire in a hearth inside an' two oul' women, one oul' woman sittin' at one side o' the fire an' another one at the other side. An' one of 'em sez across to the other one, "Oh," sez she, "they'll be here in about half an hour, an' they'll have the girl with 'em that they're bringin'. An' they'll come in a gap below there at the bottom o' the hill, an' the gap," sez she, "is facin' south from here. An' they'll be riding," sez she, "on horses, an' the girl that they're bringin' with 'em will be riding on a white horse a few yards behind the rest of 'em. An' we'll have a great dance when they come."

'An' Brian O'Brien was listening an' he thought to himself, "Faith," sez he, "they won't have her. But I'll have her."

'Out he went the tunnel an' down for John Gorman. They went up again, up the hill, John Gorman an' himself, up to the gap, an' they weren't long at the gap when the grandest-dressed lot of ladies an' gentlemen that John Gorman an' Brian O'Brien ever saw came in through the gap. An' they were all red horses they had but there was a white horse a few yards behind 'em an' a girl ridin' on that horse. When she was passin' through the gap Brian O'Brien made a jump for her an' he caught her by the leg an' pulled her down off the horse. An' when he did the whole lot of 'em turned back an' looked at himself an' John Gorman for a long time. But the two of 'em, they held her. They wouldn't give her to 'em. They brought her to Corbally House, to Mr Mahon, an' the followin' morning Mr Mahon met her. Sure, she was a dummy. She couldn't talk to him. An' she didn't speak to John Gorman or Brian O'Brien either when they were bringin' her to Corbally House. She could talk to no one.

'But, that day twelve months, November Eve again,

the music started again an' Brian O'Brien said that he'd go up to know was the same tunnel there, an' if it was he'd go in to try an' find out what was wrong with the girl that he pulled down off the horse twelve months before that.

'The music started an' John Gorman an' himself, they went up again. The same tunnel was there. Brian O'Brien went in an' he came to the same entrance to the same room. The same furniture was there. There was a big table in the middle o' the floor, an' the two oul' women, one of 'em sitting at each side o' the fire. An' one of 'em sez to the other one, an' Brian was listenin', "That thief Brian O'Brien," sez she, "took our fine girl from us this night twelve months. An' we couldn't have the dance that we were goin' to have when we hadn't the girl."

'"But," sez the other one, "she's no good to him because there's a spell over her an' she can't talk to anyone, or tell anyone her troubles."

'"But," sez the first lady then, "if she had three mouthfuls out o' that bowl on the table she'd have talk enough for him."

'She hadn't the words said out of her mouth when Brian O'Brien made a sweep in an' swept the bowl out o' the table, an' himself an' John Gorman, they went out the tunnel as fast as their legs would carry 'em an' down to Corbally House. Next morning they met her an' Brian told her that he could restore her speech with three mouthfuls out of a bowl that he brought off of a table that was inside in the tunnel under Corbally fort the night before.

'So he gave her a mouthful out o' the bowl, an' she laughed at him. He gave her another mouthful; she laughed again. An' the third mouthful she spoke an' she said she knew him.

'"Brian O'Brien from Castleconnell," sez she, "you

saved me by pullin' me off of a horse when the fairies were bringin' me to Corbally fort twelve months ago. And my father," sez she, "is in Castleconnell, an' himself an' I used to ride at the hunt in Castleconnell. An' he bought a special pony for me," sez she, "to ride at the hunts, a hunting pony. An' I'd love," sez she, "to see my father. But if you go, now, Brian O'Brien, back to Castleconnell an' tell my father that I'm here he won't believe you because," sez she, "I died in Castleconnell. That's what my father, an' everyone that knew me thinks. But I didn't die. The fairies took me, an' when the fairies take a person they leave something to resemble that person behind after 'em. An' they left something to resemble me in my place. So," sez she, "here's the only way that I can see my father. The little special hunting pony that he bought for me, he wouldn't part with that little pony," sez she, "for what gold is in Ireland. But if you can proceed to Castleconnell an' steal the pony an' bring the pony up here, after some time my father," sez she, "is going to trace that pony an' he's going to come here. And, when he comes here he'll threaten you with your life, but," sez she, "when he sees me he'll rejoice with joy an' you'll come to no harm."

'Brian O'Brien, he left Mr Mahon for a while, went down to Castleconnell, an' he wasn't long in finding out about this girl that the fairies took. He went to her father an' told him that he was lookin' for a job as a chef. Her father took him. Brian wasn't there only a few weeks when her father told him all about his daughter, how she died, about the little pony that he bought for her to ride with him at the hunts, an' he said he wouldn't part with the pony if he got what gold an' diamonds were in the world because he loved his daughter. Brian O'Brien said nothing but one night, about midnight, he got up out of his bed in Castleconnell. He went to the stable where the pony was, put on a bridle an' saddle on the pony, brought him out, an' rode him back to

Corbally.

'After some time the man in Castleconnell traced the pony to Corbally an' one day he set out to bring him back, to bring back the pony that was missin' belonging to his daughter. An' he was goin' in the avenue at Corbally when he looked in the kitchen window an' saw his daughter sitting inside at a meal at the table. He fainted when he saw her.

'Brian O'Brien an' John Gorman went out an' they brought him in an' revived him. Brian told him the whole story.

'"Well, Brian O'Brien," sez he, "you're a man amongst men. You saved my daughter, an' now you can have her as your wife."

'"Thank you very much," sez Brian.

'In a few days Brian O'Brien an' this girl that was taken by the fairies got married. According to what I heard, the whole o' the people from the County Galway, Clare an' Tipperary were at the wedding.'

'But aren't a lot o' townlands called after forts. A man below in Moohaun told me one time that the adjoining townland of Cahercoyne gets its name from a fort that's in it. An' 'tis supposed to be heard in the fort every seven years, weeping an' crying. An' that's how the townland got its name, from *cathair caoin*, or *cathair keen*, which means in English the weeping fort. 'Twould remind you a bit about what I was tellin' you about Granahan castle, wouldn't it?'

'Now, there was a family livin' in Coolacasey — 'twould be between, I'd say, Sixmilebridge an' the Windy Gap. Did you ever hear tell of it? Now, the Windy Gap is on top of a mountain an' Coolacasey is between Sixmilebridge an' that. But this family lived there, an' there was a fort on the land an' there was sand in the fort.

'Anyway, they were renovatin' the front o' the house an' plasterin' it, an' they were also makin' an avenue from the road into the house. So they went to the fort an' they took some o' the sand for the avenue. An' in a few nights after, when they'd go to bed, there used to be showers o' the sand thrown up against the windows of the house. That continued, anyway, not every night, but occasionally. An' when it continued for a few months an' had no notion o' stoppin' the man o' the house, he went to Canon Little — he was a priest in Sixmilebridge at the time — an' he told him about the showers o' sand being thrown up against the windows. An' Canon Little, he asked him to know where he got it.

'"I got it," sez he, "out of a fort that was on the land. There was no other sand in the place, only in the fort, an' I thought," sez he, "that 'twas no harm for to put it in the avenue an' around the front o' the house."

'"You know what you did?" sez Canon Little to him.

'"No!" sez he.

'"You disturbed the fairies," sez Canon Little.

'"An' who are the fairies?" sez the man to him, "or what are they?"

'"Well, I'll tell you," sez Canon Little, "who the fairies are. Now, in bygone days there did people live in those forts, an' those people that lived there, they were pagans. They knew nothing about God. But they believed in some Supreme Being, because they said to themselves, 'Who put the sun there?' and 'Who grew the grass? The trees are growin' an' what's makin' 'em grow?' They believed there was some Being doing those things, but they didn't know who or what it was. Well, those people," sez Canon Little, "they had children an' they knew nothing about baptism. Those children, they died from time to time an' they knew nothing about consecrated ground or anything like that. Consequently, they buried 'em in the fort where they lived, or around the fort outside. An' what you did," sez Canon Little, "when you brought the sand out o' the fort, you brought the remains o' their little bodies, an' you put it," sez he, "in front o' your house an' in along the avenue. An' 'tis they, now, that are throwin' the showers o' sand," sez he, "up against your windows. An' what you'll do now is this. As much as you can," sez he, "of the sand that you brought, collect it up again an' bring it back to where you got it. An' you'll find," sez he, "that that'll stop."

'Which he did. An' when he put it back, as much as he could of it, there was no more sand thrown up against his windows.'

'I have one other one for you before you go. An' I have some personal experience to tell you in this case too.

'There was a land agent below in Ballymaclune, Tom Gloster was his name, an' there was a daughter of his there, Mary. She was a very nice person. 'Twas a bungalow they were livin' in, an' at the back o' the bungalow there were two galvanised tanks; they were up on pillars, an' 'twas rainwater from the house that used to fill 'em. And, the summer of 1933 was a very, very dry summer.

'Well now, up at the back o' the bungalow — any time you go down you can see it — there's a hill, a high hill, an' on top o' the hill there's a double-ring fort. Inside in this fort there's a tunnel — I was in in the tunnel umpteen times — an' the way 'tis constructed, 'tis wider in the bottom than 'tis in the top. The walls are sloped in from the bottom, an' there are long lintels, stone lintels, across the top of it. An' then, o' course, the scraw or sod is on top o' that.

'Now, the funny part of it is that you can go in the tunnel, now, in the winter time for, I s'pose, fifteen or sixteen yards when there's a wall built across it. An' about twelve yards in, turning to the left, there's another tunnel. An' where you turn to the left you go in about two yards when there are two stone steps. Below at the bottom o' the second step in the winter time, now, there'd be about three or four inches o' water. But in the summer time, the twenty-fourth o' June, if the sun is splittin' the rocks, the water is out to the mouth of it, out to the mouth o' the tunnel. An' that's up the steps. An' the floor of it is paved with paving stones. Well now, the twenty-fourth o' December, the wetter the weather the drier 'tis. An, the drier the weather is in the summer time the wetter 'tis.

'Now, everyone down there, they use it when they have no other water for makin' tea. 'Tis good water. Lovely! I drank it.

'In 1933, anyway, every well an' stream in the place was dry, but around the mouth o' the tunnel above in the fort there was a pond o' water. And, from the people goin' in an' bringin' buckets out of it — they were goin' in there for years an' years — they had the banks o' the fort, the two banks, worn. There was a stream o' water runnin' out where they had the path worn from goin' in.

'But Mary Gloster had a workman from Daingean, an' he said to her one day in the month o' June 1933, "Look," sez he. "What I was thinkin', now, was that if the water was piped down from the fort to the tanks 'twould be ideal."

'"How well," sez she, "we didn't think of it before. We'll go to Limerick tomorrow an' we'll see about it."

'Now, the pony an' trap was their way o' travellin' that time. So they went down to Limerick an' they went into a big hardware shop an' they looked for a plumber. They got one, anyway, an' she told him that there was a fort at the back o' the house, an' there was a spring well in the fort. She said they had no water in the house for washing up or anything an' 'twas a good bit up from the house to be carryin' it in buckets, if they had it piped down to the two tanks that 'twould be ideal.

'The plumber said he'd go out to see it. So they did their messages, tackled their pony an' trap, hit for Ballymaclune, an' by the time they were just turnin' in the gate this fellow arrived after 'em on a motor bike. 'Twas the plumber. They went up to the fort, an' the plumber, he had a staff an' a rule so he took levels. He measured the depth o' the tunnel, an' from the top to the bottom was exactly four feet. He took levels, then, down to the tanks an' the bottom o' the tunnel above at the fort was twelve feet over the bottom o' the tanks. He said 'twould be ideal.

'"We'll be out in the morning," sez he, "around eleven o'clock an' we'll bring what we require."

'So, the followin' morning, anyway, her workman went up for a bucket o' water about nine o'clock, an' when he went up he might as well go out to the middle o' the field. There wasn't a drop o' water in it. He came down an' told her.

'"Is it makin' a pure joke o' me altogether you are?" she sez to him.

'"Ah, come up," sez he, "an' you'll see for yourself."

'"I won't," sez she. "I'll take your word for it."

'Eleven o'clock came. The lorry turned in the gate. The two men from Limerick, the plumber an' another fellow, got out an' the workman met 'em. He said to 'em that there wasn't a drop o' water above in the tunnel, that he went up for a bucket o' water an' there wasn't a drop in it.

'"In the name o' goodness," sez the plumber to him, "is it where there was a pond of it yesterday evenin' when I was here? Is it makin' a joke of us you are?"

'"Come up, so, an' see," sez he to the two.

'The three of 'em went up. The plumber looked at the

tunnel.

'"Have no more to do with it," sez he. "Don't touch it! Leave it as it is!"'

'From that day forward Miss Gloster wouldn't wash potatoes with the water out of it. An' the following morning 'twas running out the worn path again, out the path the people had made goin' into the fort. There was a pond of it the followin' morning around the tunnel.'

'Wait till you hear my own experience of it, though.

''Twas the end o' June 1947. I was goin' the road on the bicycle when I met, comin' down against me, a man from Ballymaclune that I knew well, an' he had a sprayin' machine an' a bucket in his hand. He pulled me up.

'"Will you come back," sez he to me, "until we fill two barrels o' water, because I'm goin' sprayin' potatoes tomorrow?"

'"All right," sez I.

'I turned back with him. We went into his place; he made tea for me, an' after the tea we got one o' those bath-pans, you know; those oval pans with the handle on both ends of it. We got that an' a bucket, an' up we went.

'We brought in our bucket an' bath-pan into the mouth o' the tunnel, an' the tunnel was about half-full. It had the second step covered goin' down to it. But, he went down, anyway, an' the second step, o' course, you could stand on it; 'twould about cover the sole of your boot. An' he used to fill the bucket an' hand it up to me an' I'd throw it into the bath-pan. We'd put about seven or eight buckets in it. An' he had two barrels outside a stone wall that was running along by the outer bank o' the fort at the southern side. The two of us, then, we'd bring out our bath-pan o' water an' empty it out over the wall into the barrel. We filled our two barrels, anyway, an' he put bluestone steeping.

'"Well," sez he, "come up to me tomorrow, around eleven o'clock, an' I'll be puttin' out that. An'" sez he, "we'll have to fill the two barrels again."

'I went away, an' next day about half past ten I arrived up an' he was puttin' out the spray on the potatoes. I started fillin' the can for him, anyway, an' when it came to about half past twelve, "Come down," sez he, "an' we'll have a drop o' tea."

'So we went down an' had the tea. He had nearly the second barrel out so he went an' finished it, an' then he sez to me, "Go down for the bath-pan now."

'I brought it up. An' he had the bucket. The two of us went in over the wall with our bath-pan an' bucket, an' when we went into the tunnel, Eddie, 'twas as dry as where we are now. An' the followin' day he told me that the same amount o' water as always was in it again. Isn't it peculiar?

'No, I never heard any explanation for it, but there was another thing I did hear about that place. A friend o' mine told me that when they were goin' to Quin school, himself an' his sisters, in the evenings when they'd be comin' home they'd go in around the fort, playing. So, 'twould be of a day in the month o' November that they went into the tunnel, an' they were runnin' in an' out in the tunnel, an' they havin' "The fairies'll catch us! The fairies'll catch us!"

'An' the next thing was, in far in the tunnel they heard what they thought was laughter. They ran out of it an' that finished 'em playin' there. An echo? Maybe it was; I don't know. You wouldn't know what to believe from young lads. But the other thing I'm after tellin' you about, the water; I saw that myself, so there's definitely something peculiar about that place.'

8. The Man who sold his Horse in Tír na nÓg

'This story was told to me by a fellow below in Moohaun. Moohaun is in the parish o' Quin, an' the story that he told me was about a man of Cahercoyne who sold a horse in Tír na nÓg. We'll call him Denis, now. Sure, didn't I know two of his grandsons well. One of 'em hurled with the old Newmarket hurling team, an' a right good hurler he was, too. But anyway, to get back to my man's story. . .

'At the time of this occurrence there used to be two horse fairs in Tulla, one in the spring time an' the other in the autumn. The spring fair would be about the last week in April, an' the autumn fair around the last week in August. I don't know which o' the fairs Denis took the horse to, but it doesn't make any difference. Now, Tulla would be about eight miles distant from where he lived, an' 'twas during the night the fairs used to be held in Tulla, or very nearly day-break in the morning anyway. But, this Denis, he put on a bridle an' saddle on the horse, I suppose about ten o'clock in the night, an' he went on the saddle an' set sail for Tulla, as the sayin' goes.

'He had gone about seven miles, he was about a mile from Tulla, when he met a man standing by the roadside who called him by his name. An' he sez, "Denis," sez he, "you're goin' to the fair o' Tulla with that fine black mare you have. What do you want for her?"

'"Forty pounds," sez Denis.

'"I'll buy her," sez the stranger to him. "Get off the saddle an' take the bridle reins in your hand, an' come after me."

'At any rate, they walked side by side for a good bit o'

117

the road, an' the stranger sez to Denis, "Come on this way," sez he.

'They turned off the road onto an avenue, or another road, an' the other road appeared to Denis to be snow-white, and Denis thought that 'twas on a white velvet carpet he was walkin'. He said to the stranger, "I was never here before, an' I'll go back."

"'Denis," sez he, "your money is sure. Follow me."

'They went a long way along this white road until they came to the entrance to a tunnel. An' when they came to the entrance to this tunnel Denis, he said to the stranger, "I'll go back," sez he, "I'll go no farther."

"'Come on," sez the stranger to Denis. "Your money is sure. Your forty pounds," sez he, "is as sure as if you had it now in your pocket. Come along with me."

'They went in the tunnel, an' after goin' in the tunnel a good way the whole place was in complete darkness. Denis said to the stranger, "I'll go back," sez he.

"'Do not. Your money is sure," sez the stranger, "your money is sure."

'They went along through the darkness, the stranger an' Denis, an' after goin' a long way they saw a light. They went on an' the light got brighter an' brighter until they came to a cross in the tunnel, one tunnel goin' to the left-hand side, an' another one goin' on straight.

"'Come on this way," sez the stranger to Denis. They turned to the left along the tunnel an' it was quite bright day-light but there was no sun. Denis looked around to see if he could see any sign o' the sun, but he could see none. They went for a long way along the tunnel until they came to a large enclosure with buildings on both sides of the enclosure. The stranger said to Denis, "You see that door there?" sez he, "the third door on your left? Go to that door," sez he, "an' open it. Bring in your horse, take off the bridle an' saddle an' hang the bridle an' saddle just inside the door on your left-hand side.

There's a peg in the wall, an' hang your saddle an' bridle on that peg. Close the door on your horse, come out again, an' follow me."

'Denis did as the stranger told him. When he came out the stranger was waitin' for him. They went back along the tunnel again, an' when they came to the junction of the tunnel the stranger sez to Denis, "Come on this way."

'They went for a long way along the tunnel which was completely lighted. They came to another large enclosure an' Denis, he saw what he never saw before. He saw golden pedestals arranged in various places around the enclosure with golden ornaments on top of these pedestals. He said to the stranger, "My good man," sez he, "I'm bewildered. I'm amazed. I'll go no farther."

'"As sure as you're there, Denis," sez he, "your forty pounds are sure. Come on with me."

'They went along the enclosure and when they came more than half way across the enclosure Denis saw at the far side a castle the like of which he never saw before. He said to the stranger, "I'll go back ," sez he.

'"Do not," sez the stranger. "Your forty pounds are sure. Come on."

'They went on through the enclosure until they came to the castle door, and that door was of solid gold. The stranger knocked at the door. A beautiful girl opened the door for them. Denis looked at her. She had a golden necklace around her neck. She had golden bracelets, one on each hand. She had a golden ring on each of her fingers. Denis looked down at her feet. She had a pair of shoes on her, low shoes, with buckles of the purest gold. Denis said to the stranger, "Who is she?"

'"Do not mind," sez the stranger, "who she is, but come on. Come on in."

'Denis an' the stranger went into the castle. Denis looked down. He saw a beautiful carpet under his feet, the sides of which were decorated with gold braid. They went along a hall until they came to the entrance to a room the door of which was of the purest gold. The stranger opened the door. He said to Denis, "Come on."

'They went into this room. The stranger said to Denis, "Sit there," sez he, "in that chair."

'Denis sat into a chair the like of which he never sat on before. The chair was padded as soft as silk an' Denis sank into it. The stranger sez to Denis, "Now," sez he, "I'll pay you for your horse."

'He went over to the far corner of the room, an' Denis looked an' saw that there was a gold safe in the corner. The stranger took a gold key out of his pocket. He opened the safe. He brought over a golden box to a table that was in the middle o' the floor. He opened the box, which was full of gold sovereigns. He counted out forty sovereigns to Denis.

'"There now, " sez he, "is the price of your horse, an' maybe," sez he, "you'd like something to eat."

'"Upon my word," sez Denis, "I would, because I'm fairly hungry."

'"All right," sez the stranger. "Come on this way."

'They went out another door out o' this room, not the door by which they went in but another door, an' when they went into the other apartment Denis was amazed an' bewildered for this apartment, 'twas long an' narrow, with a row of tables in the middle, down along this long apartment. An' at either side of the row of tables was a row of the most beautiful girls and boys that Denis ever saw. They were all about twenty years of age and when Denis saw them he was bewildered. The stranger sez to Denis, "Sit there," sez he, "in that chair an' I will bring you some food."

'Denis sat down, and when he sat down a beautiful girl that was sitting by his side, she said to him, "Do not eat anything, Denis. Refuse what you are offered."

'The stranger brought on a plate of the most delicious food that Denis ever thought he saw, an' left it before him.

'"Eat that," sez the stranger to Denis.

'"No," sez Denis. "I'm not hungry."

'"Eat that food!" sez the stranger.

'"I'm not hungry," sez Denis.

'"EAT THAT FOOD!" sez the stranger a third time.

'"No," sez Denis. "I'm not hungry."

'Immediately he said it for the third time, that he wasn't hungry, the scene was changed. Instead of the beautiful faces he saw when he entered were the most horrible and ugly creatures that he thought he ever saw. Long bony fingers were stretched towards him as if to tear him to pieces. He shuddered with fright. Immediately there was a loud crash like a crash of the loudest thunder. Immediately the whole place was plunged into darkness. Denis did not know where he was. He thought that he felt a hand grasping his hand, an' a whisper said in his ear, "Come on! Follow me."

'He was led out of the castle. The whole place was in darkness. He looked, but could see nothing. He put his hand in front of him, but the darkness was so black that he could not see it.

'"Come on," sez the stranger, "I'll save you."

'They went along. Denis did not know where he was. But then he heard a loud crash like the crash of the loudest thunder. The stranger that was bringin' him to his rescue said, "We are followed."

'Immediately Denis fainted. He thought he was lifted up by the strength of a score of people, an' carried along through the darkness. After some time he came to himself an' perceived ahead a light. The stranger brought him on, into the light, an' he looked at the stranger that brought him an' saw that 'twas the beautiful girl that opened the castle door for him, an' saw that 'twas the beautiful girl that whispered in his ear, when he was offered the food, not to eat anything. But, this girl brought him along until they came to the junction of the tunnel an' turned to the right as they were going out. She said, "Come on this way," and led him on to where the stables were. She told him, "Go over to that door there," sez she, "the third one on your left. Go in, an' your bridle an' saddle are hanging on the same peg as you hung 'em when you came in. Take the saddle an' bridle off the peg, close the door on your horse. Your horse is still there. Close the door the way the horse will not get out, an' come after me."

'He did as the girl told him. He got his bridle an' saddle an' shut the door. He came out into the enclosure again, which was the stable enclosure, an' this girl was waiting for him. And he did not know who this girl was. She said to him, "Come on quick," sez she, "we have no time to lose."

'They went back to the junction of the tunnel and turned right. When they went a long way they perceived ahead darkness, Denis did. This beautiful girl led him into the darkness, and they went a long way through the darkness, an' then ahead Denis saw daylight. They went along the tunnel until they came to where the daylight was, an' Denis looked at the girl an' he sez to her, "Who are you at all?"

'"Well, Denis," sez she, "I happen to be a grand-aunt of yours, your grand-mother's sister, who was taken by the fairies when I was only sixteen years of age. And I'm condemned to be with these," sez she, "for ever. An', Denis, if you had eaten the food you were offered when you went into that fairy castle you'd never have left it. You'd be in the same predicament as I am. You would never have got out but for me."

'"What'll happen to you when they find out that you

helped me to escape?" sez Denis.

'"Don't mind that," sez she. "Now, Denis, proceed along the avenue until you come to the side of the public road. Take care," sez she, "would you look back, or if you look back you're brought in again to the castle that I rescued you from. Take care would you look back until you come to the side of the public road. Then you can look back. Hold your saddle an' bridle firmly in your hands until you come to the side of the public road an' when you look back you'll get a surprise."

'Denis, he went along this white avenue, or white road which himself an' the stranger went in, an' the stranger was a man. When he came to the side of the public road that was at Lisofinn he looked back.

'The whole thing, the whole white road that he walked on when he went in had vanished. He was bewildered. He didn't know where he was. He was stunned. He put his hand in his trousers pocket to know had he the price of his horse, an' in his trousers pocket he found his forty gold sovereigns. He turned homewards, an', now, the man that told me the story said that Denis was the most honest man that ever lived in Moohaun, that he would not wrong anybody one penny, or ever tell a lie. He told his story to his neighbours, an' when he had it told he was so honest an' truthful that they firmly believed that he sold his black mare in Tír na nÓg, which was, according to English, the land of the youth.

'Now, I thought that was a right good story, even if there wasn't a word o' truth in it — which I think there was. I used always like to hear an interesting story an' I'd remember it if I did.

'But I asked a neighbour o' mine, Tom O'Brien, how did these fairy stories originate, or how did they come about, an' stories about ghosts an' all that.

'What Tom O'Brien told me was: the time that the five kings were in Ireland there was a king in each province, an' under these kings there were what were known as chieftains. An' a chieftain, I suppose, would be over what'd be known as a county now. An' sub-chieftains would be, I suppose, over what'd be a parish now.

'But, every year they used to hold a festival, dancin' an' singin' an' music, all the rest of it, old Irish music, an' also storytelling. Now, Tom O'Brien said that at that time maybe there was no money in Ireland an' the people, they had to pay the sub-chieftains in produce. It might be wheat or it could be cattle or something like that. But, for these festivals the people, they used to make up stories an' the best storyteller for the sub-chieftain would be forgiven maybe his rent, as I'll call it; maybe he might be forgiven so many cattle or so much wheat or something like that.

'But then the sub-chieftains, o' course, had to tell these stories to the chieftain an' the best story that'd be told to the chieftain, the chieftain would forgive the sub-chieftain something else. Then the chieftains, they had to tell the stories to the provincial king an' the king would forgive the chieftain — the best storyteller — something else. An' the provincial kings then, you see, they had to tell the stories to the high king an' the best story to the high king would maybe forgive the king something that the high king had against him.

'That's how these stories originated, and a lot of these stories weren't true at all; they were only made up. I s'pose they used to make up stories about fairies an' ghosts that were never there.

'But some of 'em were true, an' I'd say that'd be the case when the storytellers were relating something that happened to themselves or maybe someone they knew.'

9. Roguery and Nonsense

'I heard a good one from an oul' woman below in Quin one time an' it went like this:

'The day before yesterday about forty years ago I got an empty letter of an old hag's death. I was so delighted at the sad news that every tear that fell from my small toe would split six feet of rock or set a mill goin'. I got a fit of running with my two shin bones in my pockets an' my head under my arm for sixteen miles, every minute sittin' down, until I met John Dervis the coachman drivin' sixteen dead asses under an empty steam-coach loaded with two roasted mill-stones, seventeen man-o'-wars an' half-baked paving-stones. I went into Bernard Whang's an' I asked him could he give me any account or information about the shower of old hags that fell next week. He said he couldn't but John Manx could. I asked him where did John Manx live. He told me he lived in the round square house beyond all parts of the three flying asses up an' down a street where a mad dog bit a hatchet an' where the pigs fight for stirabout.

'I crossed into a small village about the size of Dublin where I saw a man running off with a load o' chimneys on his back. He had a colic on his big toe, a toothache on his shin-bone an' a headache at the back of his knee. I sent for a coach to convey him to a doctor's shop where I ordered a physic of seventeen quarts o' pigeon's milk, eighteen pounds o' frogs butter, nineteen pints of eel's beastings, seventy rogues' kidneys, a robin boiled into rags. I mixed them up together, an' I boiled them in a leathern, wooden, iron, calico pot. After he had taken the physic I brought him to a hospital where he got a fit o' coughing for eighteen days an' eighteen nights without stopping. After this he threw up strikers, seekers an' hikers, foxhounds, greyhounds, harehounds, curdogs, lapdogs an' spaniels. An' they all marched off to Saint Helena to bring back Buonaparte. They will be back on the eighty-twelfth, the hungriest month o' the year.

'There was an awful fight three weeks an' a half below Dublin between a mail-coach an' a man-o'-war, firin' boiled oyster shells, stewed lapstones an' roasted wigs at one another. An' twenty miles o' the sea got burned between them.

'I then went up in a castle eleventy twelve storeys high an' I never fell till I broke the lip-lap o' my liver against the sharp edge of a pawnbroker's wig.

'I was bidding farewell to John Dervis the coachman when he told me I should not go until he showed me more of the wonders. The first wonder he showed me was six little girls an' six little boys playing hide an' seek under a cock of hay made with stones. Another wonder he showed me was a cow going up backward a poplar tree to rob a magpie's nest. Another one that he showed me was himself an' his eldest son threshing tobacco into peas. An' one o' the peas jumped through a ditch an' killed a dead dog that was barking at a porpot cat that was dying at the other side. The ditch was only as long as 'twas Saint Patrick's Day to America. These were followed by four cripples who lost their heads armed in a dyke at the battle o' Waterloo. I thought myself to run faster than any of them, so I put my two shin-bones in my pocket an' my head under my arm an' I ran over bogs o' butter an' bog holes o' buttermilk until I came to the Curragh o' Kildare, where I struck my toe against the bridge an' knocked it down. Then the shower of oul' hags fell into the river an' got burned in the blaze o' cold water. An' now they're up in Dublin makin' straw hats out of deal boards.'

'That's what the oul' woman in Quin told me about the shower of oul' hags that fell next week. I was tellin' it

to a neighbour o' mine, an' d'you know what he told me?

'"I'll tell you how that was composed, now. 'Twas a fellow," sez he, "that got a life-sentence in jail, an' the governor o' the jail told him that if he put so many words together without any sense or meaning he'd let him go free. An' 'twas that he put together, an' the governor o' the jail let him off."

'That was the explanation that he gave me for it.'

'So, that's the finish o' my story, for the time being anyway. More? Indeed, I s'pose I have as much again that I can't think of at the moment. But, sure, what do you expect at seventy or thereabouts. 'Tisn't better the oul' head'll be gettin' with me. Anyway, I hope that some o' the stuff I told you will be of interest to someone. 'Tis no good inside my head, an' if people like it they're welcome to it. Like I told you the first time you came here, an' that's a good while ago, I like to see people lookin' forward, but 'tis a nice thing to have something to look back on too.'

Glossary

Buailtéan: the striker of a flail.

Cóiste bodhar: The Headless Coach.

Cuaird: A visit. 'On cuaird' — visiting a neighbour's house for the purpose of cardplaying, storytelling etc.

Dhera (sometimes spelt *Yerra*): Depreciative interjection, e.g. 'Dhera, don't bother going.'

Gabhlóg: A forked stick such as that used by water diviners.

Piseógs: Witchcract, practices endeavouring to gain power over the person or property of another.

Seanchaí: Teller of traditional tales.

Index of Places

THE BEDSIDE BOOK OF THE WEST OF IRELAND
Padraic O'Farrell

This is a book which will remind you of those things about the west of Ireland that you would like to remember and read over and over again.

The west of Ireland has always had a particular fascination for the native Irish and visitor alike. Its mountains, valleys, rivers, lakes and seaboard boast a visual and intellectual beauty unrivalled by any other part of Ireland — every acre echoes a legend and every stone a piece of history.

The Bedside Book of the West of Ireland takes its reader on a nostalgic journey by re-introducing us to some much loved pieces such as 'The Men of the West', 'The Boys from the County Mayo', 'Clonmacnoise', 'The Dog of Aughrim', 'Mary of Meelick', 'Westport Town', 'Lament of Mac Liag for Kincora' and 'The West's Asleep'. Padraic O'Farrell quotes some extracts from *The Book of Ballymote, The Adventures of Donnchadh Ruadh Mac Con-Mara,* Hardiman's *History of Galway* and Mr. and Mrs. C.S. Hall's *The West and Connemara* and he also gives us some fascinating information about Cormac Mac Airt, Michael Davitt, Captain Boycott and a host of other people.

The Bedside Book of the West of Ireland could truthfully be classified as a book to be taken and cherished if one had to live on a desert island.

Index of Places

THE BEDSIDE BOOK OF THE WEST OF IRELAND
Padraic O'Farrell

This is a book which will remind you of those things about the west of Ireland that you would like to remember and read over and over again.

The west of Ireland has always had a particular fascination for the native Irish and visitor alike. Its mountains, valleys, rivers, lakes and seaboard boast a visual and intellectual beauty unrivalled by any other part of Ireland — every acre echoes a legend and every stone a piece of history.

The Bedside Book of the West of Ireland takes its reader on a nostalgic journey by re-introducing us to some much loved pieces such as 'The Men of the West', 'The Boys from the County Mayo', 'Clonmacnoise', 'The Dog of Aughrim', 'Mary of Meelick', 'Westport Town', 'Lament of Mac Liag for Kincora' and 'The West's Asleep'. Padraic O'Farrell quotes some extracts from *The Book of Ballymote, The Adventures of Donnchadh Ruadh Mac Con-Mara,* Hardiman's *History of Galway* and Mr. and Mrs. C.S. Hall's *The West and Connemara* and he also gives us some fascinating information about Cormac Mac Airt, Michael Davitt, Captain Boycott and a host of other people.

The Bedside Book of the West of Ireland could truthfully be classified as a book to be taken and cherished if one had to live on a desert island.